Radical Recovery

A Manifesto of
Eating Disorder Pride

Chris Kraatz

UNIVERSITY PRESS OF AMERICA,® INC.
Lanham • Boulder • New York • Toronto • Oxford

Copyright © 2006 by
University Press of America,® Inc.
4501 Forbes Boulevard
Suite 200
Lanham, Maryland 20706
UPA Acquisitions Department (301) 459-3366

PO Box 317
Oxford
OX2 9RU, UK

Library of Congress Control Number: 2006924066
ISBN-13: 978-0-7618-3473-1 (paperback : alk. paper)

This book is dedicated to the countless people
who did not survive their disordered eating;
grandparents and parents,
siblings and spouses and friends,
children and grandchildren.
It is time to secure amends for their suffering,
and to prevent the similar suffering of others.

Contents

List of Tables

Preface

This book is not a personal "my road to recovery" narrative. It will, of necessity, contain some personal information and draw upon some personal experiences, but the purpose here is to cast a wider net and get a bigger picture. Part of the motive for making this effort stems from my own experience, but this is not a book about "me" so much as it is a book about "us." There was a time, when my eating was very disordered indeed, that I truly believed that I was alone. I was alone, of course, but not in the way that I thought. The aloneness I experienced was the result of having become isolated—a product of the curious interaction between my disordered eating and the cultural attitudes surrounding these conditions. My skewed interpretation of my loneliness, however, was that no one else was suffering as I was—I thought I was the only man who was a binge eater, severely bulimic, and anorexic. In the years that have passed since that awful time, it has occurred to me that there are many other people experiencing the same aloneness—truly alone by way of the isolating characters of disordered eating and cultural attitudes of stigma and shame, but falsely believing themselves to be the only person so suffering—and I seem to meet more eating disordered people every week who confirm in one way or another this same experience. Whence comes the question: how many of us are there?

In seeking some good information about the prevalence of eating disorders, I was routinely stumped at every turn. No person or organization, it seems, is willing to put forward any specific numbers. Prevalence estimates for other medical conditions are readily available and are fairly specific; it takes perhaps five minutes of online investigation to find out with reasonable precision how many people suffer from diabetes, cancer, AIDS, or bipolar disorder. One can even find out how many people will die next year from exposure to second hand tobacco smoke. But the estimates concerning how many people have eating disorders are uniquely vague; they are made with such a wide range of numbers as to be utterly uninformative and useless.

It seemed to me when I began this project several years ago that there had to be some kind of connection between our inner experiences of isolation and aloneness, and the fact that no one in the medical field really knows how many of us there are. It occurred to me also that if no one knew how many of us even existed, any real progress in understanding how we might recover would be nearly impossible. So I began doing some digging around on the subjects of prevalence statistics and research, while at the same time jotting down my own ideas about what life with disordered eating is like and what we might do well to tell people about our experiences. After a year or two of this conjunction of concerns, the big picture and the inner experience, this manifesto of radical recovery and pride started to come together.

Recovery really is the task at hand. It is through a collectively demanded and seized recovery for us that the lives of those who have suffered with us and not survived will be redeemed. It is through our pride and speaking out that the truth about disordered eating will be known, and the hope of preventing others from suffering will become a reality.

Readers are a gift to every author, and I thank you for taking the time to navigate through this material. If you are reading this as a healthcare provider, please do not take personally the criticisms that are directed at a system which is largely impersonal—your compassion is a necessary condition for our healing—we need you and we thank you for your interest in our conditions.

If you are reading this as a friend or family member of someone who you believe suffers from disordered eating, investing your time in these pages and other helpful resources suggests a willingness to be helpful and kind that will mean more to your person who suffers than words could express. In case they aren't "out" yet, I thank you on their behalf.

If you are reading this as a fellow eating disordered person, I embrace you—where ever you are. The time for a radical manifesto of ED pride is now. We must speak out in larger numbers and with less fear and deference to medical orthodoxy and unhealthy cultural attitudes. Let's join forces and join voices, and get heard and get better. Manifesto!

Chris Kraatz
Indianapolis, Indiana
January, 2006

Acknowledgments

Heartfelt thanks are in order for all the support I received during the writing of this book. This is most certainly a better book because of the assistance so freely given to me, and any errors or omissions are strictly my own. Owing to the potentially personal nature of much of the subject matter discussed in this book, some of the people who deserve thanks will not be mentioned here. Hopefully, I have expressed my sincere appreciation to each of you in person.

For having taken time out of their busy schedules and been willing to read the manuscript for this book, thanks very much to Amy Kuehn, William McBride, Walter Robinson, and Michelle Ruben. Your feedback and suggestions were extremely valuable, I'm blessed to have you as colleagues and friends.

For having afforded me the time and space to work on this book and the emotional support necessary to think these things through, very special thanks to my wife Linda and our son Ben—you are the best! I love you both dearly.

For having provided musical inspiration, thanks especially to Yes. I listened to the 1994 album *Talk* endlessly while writing this book and I never tired of it. *Talk* didn't receive the attention that really fine albums deserve, but many of the lyrical themes in those songs are echoed in these pages.

For spiritual support, thanks to Mother Earth for providing a firm foundation beneath my feet and continual loving sustenance for life. Thanks to the Great Mystery that surrounds and is at the center of all things.

All My Relations!

Introduction

A significant majority of the individuals currently living in the United States are "normal eaters." A normal eater is someone who observes the following general patterns of behavior:

- Tends to eat when hungry.
- Tends not to eat when not hungry.
- Eats at fairly regular intervals.
- Usually forgets about food when meals are over.
- Is able to eat a small amount of something that tastes really good.
- Avoids situations that involve starvation, vomiting, and diarrhea.

The rest of us who are not normal eaters have a very difficult time understanding how people can act this way. We can "fake it" for a while, maybe even for a long time, but we just don't get it. Try as we might, such behaviors feel unnatural to us. We marvel at how even small children know instinctively how to eat, while we remain largely ignorant of the mechanisms by which these "normal" behaviors might be induced in ourselves. We are eating disordered people. Our eating may be coerced or adjusted so as to appear normal, but our conceptual framework seems unable to accommodate that kind of thinking that would naturally produce "normal" eating.

We are anorexics—people who want to be so thin as to go virtually unnoticed by others, people who measure personal worth inversely with a scale. We intentionally starve or avoid food so as to shrink the size of our bodies as much as possible. We are binge eaters—people who are more comfortable interacting with food than with other individuals. We often eat for reasons other than physical hunger and often to the point of excess, seldom experiencing periods of time when we aren't thinking about our next meal. We are bulimics—people who cope with emotions through the use of food. We eat large amounts of food in short periods of time and then feel guilty about having overeaten, or we feel fearful about gaining weight, or we just feel and want to get rid of our feelings—so we "compensate" by throwing up our food or taking laxatives or exercising to excess.

Although more specific diagnostic criteria for disordered eating are included in the appendices to this book, the above descriptions illustrate our most common features. We have a different way of interacting with food that results largely from a different way of thinking about the world and its multitude of relationships that must be negotiated. While our thinking is merely different, however, our behavior can be very unhealthy. The ultimate purpose of this book is to facilitate, on as large a scale as possible, the recovery of people with disordered eating. In order to accomplish this task, we will of necessity have to examine the current state of affairs regarding eating disorders through a corresponding wide-angle lens. As such, this book seeks to investigate a three-way intersection of concerns; medical, political, and personal. It is obvious enough why medical issues are relevant in trying to discern the means by which people might recover from an unhealthy physical condition. But why examine the medical in deliberate connection with the political and the personal? And what do these domains have to do with recovery from disordered eating in particular?

Medically, we want to know about the prevalence and severity of disordered eating. Do these conditions exist on a scale that is "epidemic?" Do people die from disordered eating? If so, how many? What forms of effective treatment are currently available? What kind of research is currently being conducted? etc.

Politically, we want to ascertain the established practices for allocating research funds and dealing with the eating disordered as a group. Are there political factors involved in allocating research funds for these conditions? If so, what are they? What, if any, political advantages or disadvantages are present in the ways that medical authorities currently deal with eating disordered patients? Are the eating disordered "oppressed?" What would it mean to suggest such a thing?

Personally, we want to find out if there is anything that we eating disordered can contribute from our own experience that will help facilitate the recovery of ourselves and others. Do a significant portion of people who recover from disordered eating have anything in common that might be useful for other sufferers to know about? If so, what? And how can we begin sharing this personal information?

Here are the simple answers to these questions, and the central claims to be established in the pages that follow. First, the continuing large scale presence of eating disorders in the United States is attributable in significant measure to the political posturing and conduct of our major research institutions. Second, the solution to this political stale-mate in research and treatment lies in the ability of those of us who suffer or have recovered from disordered eating to bring certain personal aspects of our experience into public awareness.

One of the more notable features of the investigation being proposed is the suggestion of a new form of dialogue between those who are eating disordered and those who are not. Ideally, health care providers would be well equipped to treat patients with disordered eating to the same degree that they had an adequate understanding of what eating disordered life and recovery are like. Conversely, eating disordered patients are equipped to follow the advice of their health care providers to the same degree that they comprehend and have faith in the current methods of treatment. The dialogue which presently characterizes the relation between normal and disordered eaters is unbalanced to the point of being disadvantageous to disordered eaters; we aim to change these rules of engagement. To this end, in an effort to find common ground between the internal perspective of the eating disordered and the external perspective of the health care provider and facilitate a productive recovery-oriented discourse, an exercise in imagination is a fitting place to begin.

Imagine that you live in a world permeated by pain and misery that is directly attributable to an unhealthy medical condition; physical and mental discomfort are always in the background, and often in the foreground as well. The condition from which you suffer is epidemic. In fact, more people share your malady than any other medical condition known to exist, yet very few people acknowledge that this is so even though the condition is officially classified as an "illness" with recognized criteria for diagnosis. No one has seriously attempted to find out just how many people share your malady, and as a result very few people indeed are trying to find out how to alleviate your painful and life-threatening symptoms. Most people in the general population are vaguely aware that such "sickness" exists somewhere, but when people find out that someone has this condition they tend only to respond with ridicule, disgust, fear, and pity. Media attention regarding your condition is focused solely on celebrities who have died and the resulting jokes of questionable taste told by comedians and talk show hosts. Despite the wide-spread cultural and social pressures which have been demonstrated to trigger your unhealthy condition, reporters and academics spend more time demonizing sufferers who are publicly self-affirming than they do criticizing the known causes of the suffering. So, when people manifest this condition they try not to tell anyone. You suspect that others suffer as you do, but you've never actually spoken to another person who admits it. You've attempted to communicate with other sufferers online, but web-sites which facilitate such discourse are routinely shut down by people who accuse them of "promoting" an unhealthy life-style. Health care providers attempt to treat people who, by virtue of their deteriorating health, can no longer hide the fact that they have this condition—often against their wishes. But since research that might help find solutions is poorly funded, the treatments are mostly ineffective and often even make the symptoms worse. Despite the lack of research funding and efficient treatments, many healthcare providers continue to insist that people with your condition "just make very bad patients." As a result of all this, you're more frightened by the prospect of being treated than you are about dying. And dying is a very likely outcome, since the condition you have is more deadly than most known illnesses.

Those of us with eating disorders live in this world.

Current work in the area of eating disorders may seek to accomplish many interesting and revealing ends, but if little or nothing is done to facilitate recovery, then the work is ultimately useless to us. Recovery for all of us is the number one priority, but within the present climate of treatment options we don't seem to recover very much (or at least not for very long periods of time). This means that we need a model for recovery that is radical.

In this context, we are employing all of the meanings commonly associated with the term "radical." Of course, we mean to suggest moving in a direction that is significantly different from what has traditionally been done in the failed attempt to account for, research, understand, and facilitate the healing of disordered eating. Something about how we understand eating disorders and recovery is seriously flawed. The need radically to depart from accepted eating disorders orthodoxy is proportional to that orthodoxy's inability to serve our needs—and that inability is significant.

Radical, in this context, also indicates the relation between a disease and a cure—radical is in fact a medical term. A radical cure is one which gets to the root of an illness; a radical procedure is one which gets to the ultimate source of a malady. Of course, making these points inevitably leads to the question of why an approach to our healing that is medically radical must, at one and the same time, be conceptually radical. If radical healing is complete, then why is it a radical suggestion that we be healed in this way? Why is complete healing for us a deviation from traditional medicine as we know it? Why are the suggestions that we construct reliable prevalence estimates and improve our recovery rates unusual suggestions? In the chapters that follow, we will have to address in some way the matter of our having been relatively ignored for a very long time.

Whence comes the requirement of manifesto. I use the word here as a verb rather than as a noun. Linguistically, this is not too much of a stretch. The

Latin word *manifestus* (from which we get the English manifesto) literally means blatant, flagrant, or obvious. *Manifestus* suggests being caught in the act for all to see. A written work that is a manifesto is usually understood to be a public declaration of principles, intentions, motives, or objectives—and this work is a manifesto in that sense. But manifesto applies in the original Latin context at least as much, insofar as we are trying to bring some things out into the open.

What needs to be out in the open for all to see in order to facilitate our radical recovery? To begin with, and at the very least, we need to call out those institutions that have been charged with responsibilities of healthcare—they have been and continue to be severely derelict in their accepted duties. The neglect of disordered eating in nearly all aspects of research and treatment in the United States constitutes a serious blemish on this system, a national failure the enormity of which cannot be over-stated. Based on what we shall present in the chapters that follow, it would be difficult to defend the current state of such research and treatment as anything less than a deliberate refusal to prevent millions of citizens from suffering and dying. I realize that this claim sounds extreme, but it will be justified by the information presented here.

What else needs to be out in order to make radical recovery a reality? Well, we need to be out. To be sure, we need to make blatant and obvious the negligence of those who have failed to take our health into account. At the same time, however, we have to stop contributing to their ignorance by never speaking of our conditions. If we don't speak up, then how is anyone supposed to learn that we exist and what disordered eating is really about? Externally, manifesto means calling out those public institutions that are corrupt and negligent and disclosing them for what they are—shameful. Internally, manifesto means coming out and demanding that our needs be recognized—with pride. Both these dynamics of manifesto must work in tandem, one without the other will not further the cause of our radical recovery—as we now know from our painful and prolonged experiences.

As well, the issue of shame or stigma threatens to undermine our recovery if not properly put in its place. What shame accomplishes is the keeping silent of the person on whom it is placed; no one wants to come out only to disclose to others their own shame. So long as we are ashamed of ourselves or embarrassed by our conditions, our ability to recover is stifled because we are less inclined to speak up, and therefore less inclined to get what we need. Since manifesto that facilitates radical recovery is necessarily shame free, we need to let our pride find meaningful expression. This does not mean that we celebrate the fact that our physical health is threatened by disordered eating, but it certainly implies that we need to come to celebrate something about the fact that we are eating disordered. There is something about our "disordered" way of relating to the world that is quite valuable, good, and worth celebrating — and we will try to come to an understanding of what that something is. At the very least, pride means that we do not regard our eating disorders as personal flaws or indicators of immorality, sin, or mental defect. "Illness" is a label that applies to our disordered eating behaviors, but it does not apply to the psychological constitutions from which our behaviors arise.

The outline then for this work proceeds as follows. In the first chapter, we'll count heads; find out just how many of us there are in this country. This is no easy task, as it necessarily involves consulting a wide variety of sources in order to piece together a reasonably accurate prevalence estimate. This initial chapter, therefore, includes more attention to technical medical research than perhaps other portions of the book. As well, we will address the question of severity in this section, noting specifically the mortality rates associated with disordered eating. The findings presented in this chapter are overwhelming indeed, and it is expected that authorities in the field of eating disorders orthodoxy will reject this chapter out of hand. It may be a surprise to some people to learn that there are more people with disordered eating than any other known medical condition. We will offer conclusive proof, however, that there is no sufficient justification for rejecting this claim — this first chapter presents information that is based directly on widely recognized and current research.

In the second chapter we'll address the question of what is being done about the epidemic of disordered eating in the United States. Our focus here will be on the principal research institutions responsible for gathering and disseminating information in the field of eating disorders, and currently available forms of treatment and their rates of success. Although disordered eating affects more Americans than any other illness and claims a staggering number of lives each year, current research in this field remains virtually unfunded. This chapter will examine current trends in research and outline their notable effects on treatment options and the training of healthcare providers.

The third chapter explains why it is that people with disordered eating need to speak out, this is the call for manifesto. Upon finding our prevalence and mortality to be astoundingly high and yet the current state of research and treatment to be appallingly poor, we find it necessary to take matters into our own hands and enter into discourse with each other, with others who are normal eaters, and with our healthcare providers. Since our silence only serves to maintain an already unacceptable status quo, our speaking out about what it's like to be eating disordered will provide the means for change and, ultimately, the recovering of good health for us all.

The fourth chapter is an example of such speaking out. It is not a narrative that details my personal experiences with disordered eating, but is rather a phenomenology of eating disordered experience as such. Narratives tend to focus on the content of experience, but the basic form or structure of eating disordered experience wants also to be understood. If we could discern a common conceptual framework from which disordered eating behaviors emerge, we would be in a better position to make suggestions about how recovery might be facilitated. The basic thrust of this chapter is to place our focus on the ways that we eating disordered people interact with and relate to the world around us—something about that interaction is fundamentally unique to the eating disordered perspective.

In the fifth chapter, we will argue that while the behaviors by which we are diagnosed are very unhealthy, the perspective from which we view the world is in fact useful and good; "disordered eating" may be an illness, but being "eating disordered" can be a very positive quality of character indeed. In acknowledging that who we are is not to be strictly identified with what we do, we can concede the imperative to change our actions while at the same time taking pride in the perspective from which they emerged—this is ED pride ("ED" is a common abbreviation for "eating disorder"). In order fully to express this pride and raise the public awareness of our situations, some strategies for direct action—protests—are offered in this chapter as well.

Finally, in the concluding section of the book, we'll offer some concrete constructive ideas about what should be done differently at all levels of eating disorders research and treatment. In the spirit of other manifestos in written history, these ideas will be presented as demands; changes that are necessary for us to insure our survival.

Underlying this strategy as it's been laid out is the idea that we have to work together to achieve these ends. The "we" is us; eating disordered people. I know from my own experience that it's all too easy to lose sight of one's connection to other disordered eaters, especially when the culture we live in discourages speaking out about such things. To the extent that we come together, however, we will be able to gain some long overdue access to adequate healthcare. Moreover, to the extent that we demand appropriate respect for ourselves we restore a measure of dignity to those who didn't survive their disordered eating. Remember, those who have died from disordered eating are *our* dead, we are them and they are us.

Chapter One

Prevalence and Mortality: How Bad Is It, Really?

Initially, the question of prevalence is of foremost concern. After all, if only a handful of people suffer from some particular illness, syndrome, or condition, that's no great cause for panic. If such a circumstance is found to prevail in epidemic proportions, however, that calls for a very different response indeed. Responding appropriately to disordered eating necessitates that at some point we ask the question of how many eating disordered people there are. The mere asking of this question, however, seems automatically to involve one in a radical approach to understanding these conditions. Although there are many speculative figures available in response to this most basic question, the issue of prevalence is seldom taken up in a serious or diligent manner in connection with eating disorders. Unfortunately, current prevalence estimates are vague, and many are offered with disclaimers attached to them.

Even the most recognized national organizations whose purpose it is to distribute information about eating disorders are reluctant to boast any specific answers to the question of prevalence. This is a typical example, from the National Eating Disorders Association:

> In the United States, as many as 10 million females and 1 million males are fighting a life and death battle with an eating disorder . . . many cases are probably not reported.[1]

No less than four different books and one article (all more than 10 years old) are referenced in order to substantiate this ambiguity, none of which makes any mention of a survey inquiry which asks whether or not one's eating disorder is a "life and death battle."[2] One gets the impression that the numbers are supposed

1

to look more precise by virtue of the excessive citations. This next one speaks for itself, from Anorexia Nervosa and Related Eating Disorders, Inc.:

> In a study reported in Medscape's *General Medicine* 6(3) 2004, prevalence rates in Western countries for anorexia nervosa ranged from 0.1% to 5.7% in female subjects. Prevalence rates for bulimia nervosa ranged from 0% to 2.1% in males and from 0.3% to 7.3% in female subjects . . . Because physicians are not required to report eating disorders to a health agency . . . we have no way of knowing exactly how many people in this country are affected . . . Now, that having been said, the journal Clinician Reviews [13(9) 2003] estimates that each year about five million Americans are affected by an eating disorder. But there is disagreement."[3]

Indeed there is disagreement. Here is one such dissenting opinion, from the National Institute of Mental Health (in consultation with the American Psychiatric Association):

> An estimated 0.5 to 3.7 percent of females suffer from anorexia nervosa in their lifetime. An estimated 1.1 percent to 4.2 percent of females have bulimia nervosa in their lifetime.[4]

This estimate has all the appearance of a precise answer to the question of prevalence, until one consults the United States Census Bureau's data from the 2000 census; there are 144 million females in the United States. According to the data that the NIMH is willing to accept, anorexia affects somewhere between 750,000 and 5.3 million women, bulimia affects somewhere between 1.6 million and 6 million women. Thus the NIMH prevalence estimate for these disorders is somewhere between 2.35 million and 11.3 million people.

Not only are the NIMH and *General Medicine* estimates at notable odds with one another (the anorexia estimate of the latter is roughly half that of former), but their huge range and lack of data pertaining to men or eating disorders other than bulimia and anorexia—such as "eating disorder not otherwise specified" (EDNOS), pica, or rumination, for example, all of which have recognized criteria for diagnosis which are listed in the appendices at the end of this book—cast serious suspicion on the meaning and usefulness of these numbers. The National Institutes of Health (of which the NIMH is a member) has boasted for years about its ability to predict with enviable precision the number of people who will die of exposure to second hand smoke in a given year.[5] Yet this same government institution is either unable or unwilling to present any reasonably specific estimate as to the prevalence of eating disorders.

Admittedly, part of the problem associated with determining the prevalence of eating disorders has to do with the quasi-established diagnostic criteria for these illnesses. In the United States, the *Diagnostic and Statistical*

Manual for Mental Disorders (DSM-IV) provides the standard criteria for diagnosis of an eating disorder, but there are still problems in this regard. One of the problems is that this manual is not recognized in the international medical community with the primacy it is accorded in the United States.

The International Statistical Classification of Diseases and Related Health Problems (ICD-10) published by the World Health Organization is often used in Europe rather than the DSM-IV. While the more general features of eating disorders are described similarly in these two manuals, many of the diagnostic details are inconsistent—this makes cross-cultural comparisons of prevalence (such as the *GM* article cited above) nearly impossible to verify. To further complicate matters, the Nation Health Service (which is the United Kingdom's rough equivalent of the NIH, providing services to England, Scotland, Wales, and Northern Ireland) has its own "Primary Care Protocols" which is used for the diagnosis of eating disorders, and the Protocols only includes criteria for anorexia and bulimia (see appendices for complete diagnostic criteria from each of these manuals). The result of this plurality of criteria is that one and the same set of symptoms conceivably could result in several very different diagnoses depending on the diagnostic preferences and country of origin of the diagnosing physician.[6]

This situation of diagnostic "flexibility" need not, however, dissuade us from attempting to determine a specific answer to the question of the prevalence of eating disorders. Even though the criteria allow for one set of symptoms to receive several different diagnoses, they seem to agree on the broader matter of whether or not an individual is eating disordered at all. Bulimic-like symptoms, for example, might receive different specific labels in different systems, but all widely used diagnostic manuals would provide the basis for some kind of "eating disordered" diagnosis. The systems have different ways of categorizing eating disorders, but they seem to be dealing with the same general domain.[7]

Our goal in this section, then, is to construct a reliable account of how many eating disordered people there are in the United States. Although the concluding section of this book contains detailed suggestions for revising the diagnostic criteria currently offered in the DSM-IV, for the sake of maintaining consistency with current research we will rely upon the current DSM-IV criteria for information regarding anorexia, bulimia, and EDNOS.

It is evident that the overall prevalence of eating disorders in the United States has not been (and perhaps cannot be) determined from the results of any one single study. We can, however, construct a reasonably specific and accurate estimate of how many eating disordered people there are in the United States by consulting a variety of studies specifically designed to answer this question for smaller or more focused populations. We will then consolidate that information into a figure that presents a generalized picture of prevalence.

Data from the United States Census Bureau will prove helpful in this regard. If we are able, for example, to determine the prevalence of eating disorders in a specific age group or otherwise identifiable segment of the population, and if the census data tell us how many people are in that group nationally, then we can calculate the number of eating disordered people in that segment of the population nationally. By consulting a variety of studies that provide figures for as many non-overlapping segments of the population as possible, we can piece together a prevalence estimate that is more comprehensive and specific than those which are currently available.[8] We might point out as well that the census data being consulted are five years old at the time of this writing, adding credence to the notion that our emerging estimate will remain fairly conservative.

To begin, there are several good studies concerning prevalence in younger age groups. In order to provide a statistical context for these studies, we will set them against the backdrop of the following figures from the most recent census. According to the data from the 2000 census, the United States population age 10 to 14 years is 20.6 million; for ages 15 to 19 years the population is 19.9 million. Women and men are almost evenly split, constituting 51 percent and 49 percent of the overall population, respectively. We have, then, about 41 million people between the ages of 10 and 19; approximately 21 million females and 20 million males.[9]

In one particularly large study which focused on the 10–14 age group, a "Youth Risk Behavior Survey" was given to about 7,000 middle school students.[10] Of specific interest on the survey were questions regarding the use of diet pills, as well as vomiting and laxative use. Results showed that 7.1% of these students used vomiting and laxatives as weight loss methods. Since there are 20.6 million people in this age group nationally, this study suggests that there are about 1.5 million children between the ages of 10 and 14 in the United States who are within the general guidelines of the diagnostic criteria for bulimia.[11]

To be sure, use of laxatives and vomiting does not constitute a sufficient condition for diagnosis of an eating disorder, and this is why we have refrained from equating the two and have rather taken this study as "suggestive." Use of laxatives and vomiting does suggest something, or else such use wouldn't be part of the accepted criteria for diagnosis. What we have pointed out here is that a certain number of people have been found to display accepted symptoms for diagnosing eating disorders. Also of relevance in this regard is that our estimate for this group does not include any numbers for anorexia. So, even if 1.5 million is an overstated estimate specifically for bulimia prevalence, the fact that anorexics are clearly left out serves to attenuate the estimate. This estimate is obviously incomplete on the one hand, and may be somewhat overstated on the other—given the relatively small figure we are here presented with, we can safely regard this estimate as reasonable and balanced.

The younger portion of the 15–19 age group shows a similar prevalence of eating disorders for males, but a sharp increase for females. The recent study which demonstrates this was significantly more detailed than the one referenced in connection with the 10–14 age group, providing prevalence figures for each of the different DSM-IV eating disorders diagnoses.[12] In this study, about 2,000 adolescents age 14–15 completed the Survey for Eating Disorders (this survey includes DSM-IV diagnoses for all subcategories of eating disorders). The results showed a 6.5 percent prevalence of eating disorders among the boys (0.2% anorexia, 0.4% bulimia, 0.9% binge eating disorder, 5.0% eating disorder not otherwise specified), and a 17.9 percent prevalence for girls (0.7% anorexia, 1.2% bulimia, 1.5% binge eating disorder, 14.6% eating disorder not otherwise specified). Assuming that these figures hold for the 15–19 age group generally, this study suggests that about 650,000 boys and 1.8 million girls in this age group meet the DSM-IV criteria for some eating disorder.[13]

Based on these two studies, we can conservatively say that there are about *4 million* eating disordered people in the United States between the ages of 10 and 19, roughly 10% of that segment of the population. To put this in perspective, the NIMH prevalence estimate (mentioned above) which covers all age groups suggests a minimum of 2.35 million females as anorexic or bulimic. Our analysis here shows that this figure is easily eclipsed within our child and adolescent population alone.

It is clear that the minimum NIMH prevalence estimates are unrealistic. We may, therefore, find the NIMH figures more useful if we lean towards the center of what they suggest. Specifically, in estimating that "0.5 to 3.7 percent of females suffer from anorexia nervosa in their lifetime," the mean estimate given is 2.1 percent. Also, the "estimated 1.1 percent to 4.2 percent of females [who] have bulimia nervosa in their lifetime" provides a mean estimate of 2.65 percent.[14] This "middle of the road" figure suggests a 4.75 percent lifetime prevalence of anorexia and bulimia (combined) for females. This mean estimate from the NIMH is clearly preferable to the minimum estimate because the minimum has already been exceeded in the 10–19 age group alone. It is also preferable insofar as we are avoiding the maximum estimates and the inflated numbers that they might produce. Having determined the most realistic and prudent prevalence statistics that the NIMH is willing to stand by, we are now in a position to determine the lifetime prevalence for anorexia and bulimia for females outside the 10–19 age group.

Turning our attention once again to the 2000 census, we find that outside the 10–19 age group there are 122 million females in the United States; 4.75 percent of this group is 5.8 million people. We have so far found that a total of about *9.8 million* people are eating disordered according to the DSM-IV criteria. Moreover, we have yet to include estimates for males outside the 10–19 age group, and we have yet to include estimates for binge eating disorder and other EDNOS diagnoses (male and female) outside the 10–19 age group.

The NIMH prevalence estimates we've used so far are indexed specifically to females, so we'll have to turn elsewhere to include males in our overall figure. Fortunately, the *GM* report (cited above) provides information concerning bulimia prevalence among males. Although the *GM* report provides us with a much wider range than does the NIMH report (also noted earlier), the mean estimates provided by the *GM* report are very close to the NIMH mean estimates (at least with regard to prevalence among females). To be consistent, then, we can calculate the number of bulimic males (outside the 10–19 age group) by using the mean estimate from the *GM* report; "Prevalence rates for bulimia nervosa ranged from 0 percent to 2.1 percent in males."[15] The mean of the *GM* prevalence estimate for bulimia in males is 1.05 percent.

According to the United States Census Bureau information for the year 2000, there are about 118 million males (not including the 10–19 age group). 1.05 percent of this population is about 1.2 million males. Add these 1.2 million bulimic males to our previous total of 9.8 million (anorexic and bulimic females, and male and female eating disordered persons in the 10–19 age group), and we are now at a conservative total of *11 million* eating disordered persons in the United States. We still have yet to include anorexic males and binge eaters (and, more broadly, those with an EDNOS diagnosis) outside the 10–19 age group.

We will derive an account of how many anorexic males there are in the following manner. In keeping with our effort to use conservative and yet widely accepted data, the baseline for this part of our estimate will be the NIMH accepted figure that roughly 10 percent of the anorexics in the United States are males.[16] This, of course, means that female anorexics account for about 90 percent of the anorexic population in the United States. According to our previous finding, there are approximately 2.6 million anorexic females in the United States.[17] Assuming that this accounts for about 90 percent of the anorexic population, we find that there are approximately 300,000 anorexic males in the United States. Thus, our total has reached *11.3 million* eating disordered persons.

Estimating the number of people with a diagnosis of EDNOS is much more difficult due to the wide ranging criteria for establishing this diagnosis which we have previously discussed. To be sure, those with binge eating disorder will fall into this category, but so will others who are not binge eaters. The DSM-IV provides, for example, a diagnosis of "eating disorder not otherwise specified" for persons meeting all the anorexia criteria except low body weight, as well as for persons meeting all the bulimia criteria except having engaged in "compensatory" behavior for at least 3 consecutive months.

We will begin our count of the EDNOS population (again, outside of the already counted 10–19 age group) by attempting to tally the binge eaters. There are usable (NIMH accepted) statistics in this regard, suggesting that 3.5 percent of the total United States population suffers from this disorder.[18] The total United States population according to the 2000 census (and not including the 10–19 age group) is 240 million. Hence, the number of binge eaters to be added into our count is 8.4 million. This brings our total number of eating disordered people to *19.7 million*, according to a conservative analysis of widely accepted data.

We must finally account for those people who merit a diagnosis of EDNOS but are not counted as binge eaters. We are here entering upon terrain which has been the subject of fewer and fewer studies. "Sub-threshold" or "partial" eating disorders have not been recognized as widely or for as long a time as have their more severe manifestations, but they can be diagnosed according to criteria given in the DSM-IV. Moreover, current data are available that will help suggest a very conservative estimate for these disorders. According to one recent study, there are twice as many people suffering from the sub-threshold bulimia-type EDNOS than there are those who merit an actual diagnosis of bulimia.[19] In order to establish the most widely acceptable and least arguable estimate possible, and since there are precious few studies that can confirm this 2:1 ratio, let us operate under the assumption that the number of "sub-threshold" or "partially eating disordered" persons is merely equal to the number of actual anorexics and bulimics. We established earlier that there are 5.8 million female anorexics and bulimics (not including the 10–19 age group), and 1.5 million males of the same description.[20] This places our estimate of the EDNOS population at 7.3 million people, thus bringing our total estimate of eating disordered persons in the United States to *27 million*.

It is important to note that this figure still does not include a great many eating disordered people. We have made no attempt here to determine how many people meet the diagnostic criteria for rumination or pica, for example, even though recent studies suggest that there are likely several million more people who fit these diagnoses.[21] Moreover, our data for the 10–14 age group did not include the necessary information for estimating a prevalence statistic for anorexia within that group. Given the notable and obvious incompleteness of this count, therefore, along with our persistent avoidance of inflated figures (by using only mean estimates provided by the NIMH as well as somewhat antiquated census data), we have established a prevalence estimate for eating disorders in the United States that is reasonable by all accepted standards — *27 million people.*[22]

To fully understand the enormity of this prevalence estimate, we need to provide some context in which these numbers can have meaning. 27 million sounds like a huge number, and indeed it is a huge number, but it is just a number until it is related to other meaningful elements of our understanding and experience. Without a familiarity of what sorts of numbers apply to the other areas of life, one might well ask: "27 million people? Is that a lot?" Of course, we can begin to get a handle on how many people are eating disordered by noting that diagnosable eating disorders affect about one out of every ten people in the United States. We could point out that, given the conservative nature of our estimate, the eating disordered population in the United States very likely exceeds the entire population of Canada. While such comparisons are helpful in some respects, what we really need to know is how the prevalence estimate for eating disorders compares to the prevalence estimates for other diagnosable conditions. Only with this information will we be equipped to evaluate the comparative magnitude of eating disorders prevalence.

As part of the Fiscal Year 2005 Hearing on Substance Abuse and Mental Health, Thomas R. Insel, M.D., Director of the National Institute of Mental Health, offered testimony to the House Subcommittee on Labor-HHS-Education Appropriations (April 29, 2004). During his testimony, Dr. Insel indicated to the House Subcommittee that some of the specific conditions which come under the purview of the NIMH deserve to be considered as "major diseases" or "serious mental illnesses." The Director's list in this regard included Alzheimer's disease, anxiety disorders, autism, bipolar disorder, major depression, schizophrenia, and eating disorders.[23]

It is interesting to note that prevalence is tracked with meticulous detail in connection with each of these conditions researched by the NIMH, except eating disorders. This tracking is accomplished though a variety of mechanisms (detailed in the corresponding notes below), and produces an overall picture of prevalence for each of these conditions that is relatively comprehensive and specific. As a consequence of this, these major mental illnesses are widely accepted as prevailing according to the statistics in table 1.1, to which we will add our eating disorders statistic.

The really striking feature of this picture, of course, is the huge prevalence of eating disorders in comparison to all the other conditions considered "ma-

Table 1.1.   National prevalence of major
mental illnesses

Illness	Prevalence
Alzheimer's Disease	4 million cases[24]
Anxiety Disorders	19 million cases[25]
Autism	1.5 million cases[26]
Bipolar Disorder	2.3 million cases[27]
Eating Disorders	27 million cases
Major Depression	18.8 million cases[28]
Schizophrenia	2.2 million cases[29]

jor" and/or "serious" by the NIMH Director. Indeed, of the 74.8 million total cases of such "major mental illnesses," fully 36 percent are eating disorders. "Major disease" will have to give way to "epidemic" in light of this fact that eating disorders comprise more than one third of all major "mental illnesses" in the United States.

An even greater sense of the magnitude of eating disorders prevalence can be gained by juxtaposing our 27 million cases against the backdrop of other conditions outside the field of mental illness. For example, in 2004 there were 1.3 million cancer cases diagnosed (a total of 18 million cases were diagnosed between 1990 and 2004).[30] There were also 700,000 stroke victims in 2004 (there are 5.4 million stroke survivors).[31] There were 1.2 million heart attacks in 2004 (and there are 7.1 million heart attack survivors).[32] There are currently about 16 million people living with diabetes.[33] By way of these figures, we are left with the astonishing realization that the number of eating disordered people is nearly as high as the 15 year total number of cancer diagnoses, all living survivors of heart attacks, and all living survivors of strokes *combined*. One wonders what other evidence would be needed in order to argue that eating disorders do not constitute merely one of the major diseases, but rather THE major disease.

Given the overwhelming picture that our conservative prevalence estimate has generated, the question which really wants to be asked is "why weren't we counted sooner?" Think about it—we eating disordered outnumber the sufferers of every other known disease in the United States. And yet, the best estimates that we get (from the NIMH on down to the non-profit awareness organizations) is the absurdly vague claim that a few million people suffer from an eating disorder. That's it. It is alleged that "people with eating disorders often do not recognize or admit that they are ill."[34] Apparently, no one else does either.

At this point, the skeptical minded may be inclined to point out that although forced to admit that our numbers are great, it does not follow from this alone that our condition is as severe as we are suggesting. The other diseases we've mentioned in comparison (i.e., Alzheimer's, schizophrenia, cancer, heart attack, diabetes, etc.) are obviously associated with acute and protracted suffering. Certainly (the skeptic might intimate) we've painted too grim a picture, the harsh quality of these other diseases outweighs the sheer quantity of eating disorders. This claim, however, that eating disorders are less severe than the other illnesses mentioned, would be impossible to defend in light of recent studies concerning mortality rates.

Much of the information that would be useful in this context simply hasn't been collected yet. In part, the lack of information on mortality rates of eating disorders can be explained by the difficulty of trying to separate eating disorders from the many other illnesses of which they are known to be a contributing causal factor. Binge eaters, for example, may well end up with cardiovascular disease as a direct result of their disordered eating. But if such a person should die of a heart attack, the cause of death would not (statistically) be counted in the mortality assessment of binge eating disorder. There are many such illnesses with high mortality rates to which eating disorders contribute in this way, but for which there is no feasible way concretely to separate the deaths ultimately attributable to an eating disorder from those attributable to other causes.[35]

Lack of information on mortality rates of eating disorders is also attributable to a simple lack of research. We know, for example, that bulimics are at a greatly increased risk for cardiomyopathy (especially resulting from ipecac poisoning), gastric and esophageal rupture, pulmonary aspiration, and even rectal prolapse. While all of these conditions have exceptionally high mortality rates, there are no data at present to suggest what proportion of bulimics actually suffer such a fate or how many of the deaths that occur from these conditions are attributable to an eating disorder.[36]

The most widely recognized and meticulously documented work in this regard is that of Patrick Sullivan. In fact, Dr. Sullivan's work has provided the primary data from which the National Institute of Mental Health has constructed its understanding of mortality and eating disorders. What lends credence to Sullivan's findings is that they are drawn from a multitude of studies that have been conducted over a long period of time by a great many people. Sullivan's work serves as a consolidation and synthesis of years of experimental work and data collection, providing perhaps for the first time a comprehensive picture of the lethal nature of anorexia. In 1995, Sullivan analyzed results from 42 different published studies concerning long-term outcome for patients with anorexia.[37] His findings were not only astonishing, but have been replicated by subsequent studies (conducted by himself as well as others). Specifically, Sullivan's 1995 study concludes that the mortality rate for anorexia nervosa is 5.6 percent per decade.[38]

What this number means is that every 10 years, 5.6 percent of anorexic people die as a direct result of their eating disorder. Given 100 people struggling with anorexia today, about 6 of them will be dead within 10 years, after 20 years about 11 of them will be dead, 17 will be dead after 30 years, 22 of them will be dead in 40 years, etc. Again, the numbers by themselves can seem misleadingly small. Keep in mind that the average age of onset for anorexia is 14–18 years of age.[39] Thus, 22 percent of anorexics are dead before they reach their mid-50s.

Taking these numbers at face value (as the NIMH has seen fit to do), we can find out how many people in the United States die each year from anorexia. According to our preceding estimate, there are about 3 million anorexic people in the United States today.[40] At a mortality rate of 5.6 percent per decade, 10 years from now 168,000 of our anorexics will be dead. That's 16,800 deaths *per year* from anorexia.

This horrendous discovery is taken as evidence by many that anorexia is the most lethal of all psychiatric disorders. Sullivan's work in this regard is widely cited, perhaps most notably by the NIMH which asserts that:

> The mortality rate among people with anorexia has been estimated at 0.56 percent per year, or approximately 5.6 percent per decade, which is about 12 times higher than the annual death rate due to all causes of death among females ages 15–24 in the general population.[41]

Along with this finding of extreme mortality, the chronic nature of eating disorders is being documented as well. Anorexia is now known to be the third most common chronic illness for adolescent girls.[42]

One recent study published in the *Journal of the American Medical Association* (and notably cited by the Centers for Disease Control and Prevention) claims that annual death rates for underweight individuals are staggering. According to this study, in the year 2000 there were more than 33,000 deaths which resulted from being underweight.[43] The conclusions which can be drawn from this finding are somewhat limited if for no other reason than that the study does not indicate how many people might die of anorexia due to complications other than being underweight (such as cardiac arrest, for example, which can result even if someone has been returned to a "normal" weight). There are a multitude of life-threatening complications which can result from anorexia besides being underweight. Thus this study is certainly consistent with our finding above that anorexia kills 16,800 people yearly.

Occasionally, it is a straightforward matter to show that skeptical readers are simply unfamiliar with the literature which has recently emerged. One "expert" reviewer of this chapter took particular exception to my assertion that the *JAMA* article (cited above) is consistent with the claim that anorexia kills 16,800 people annually. The basis for the reviewer's skepticism was that the article clearly indicates that "[O]f the 33,746 estimated excess deaths associated with underweight, the majority, 26,666 excess deaths, occurred in individuals aged 70 years and older."[44] This leaves only 7,080 excess deaths associated with underweight in individuals less than 70 years of age, which was alleged by the reviewer to be inconsistent with claiming that 16,800 people die annually from anorexia. But, of course, this is only a problem if we assume that the prevalence of anorexia is significantly lower among the elderly. In the absence of this assumption, this study's entire 33,000+ annual deaths due to being underweight are fair game for alleging consistency with our (comparatively modest) estimate of 16,800. The reviewer in fact assumed precisely this in stating of the elderly that they "have a totally miniscule prevalence of anorexia."[45]

Recent studies, however, with which any authority on eating disorders should be familiar, indicate that this is not the case—there is no good reason for thinking that prevalence is less among the elderly, and there is plenty of evidence that prevalence among the elderly is quite high indeed. One study which is particularly detailed and explicit about this aspect of anorexia mortality indicates the following:

> [R]esults showed a higher than expected age at the time of death. Specifically, a substantial percentage (43.9%) of deaths [attributable to anorexia nervosa] occurred among individuals older than 65 years . . . the diagnosis of anorexia nervosa is especially vulnerable to misclassification in the elderly due to poor nutritional status and decreased energy intake often exhibited during the aging process. Several medical conditions associated with older age can affect appetite regulation, as can a variety of prescription medications and sundry social, psychological and physiologic factors. . . "anorexia," or loss of appetite, may be poorly distinguished from "anorexia nervosa" by those responsible for medical records or death certificates . . . it can be speculated that older individuals comprise a significant portion of nontreated eating disorder populations, possibly due to underrecognition or misclassification of symptoms, or a lack of access to services. The acknowledgement that a serious eating disorder can occur at any age might stimulate better detection of nontraditional clinical presentations.[46]

Although this study is notably explicit in its articulation of anorexia mortality in the elderly, it is by no means the only study to indicate this trend. There are so many other recent publications (case studies and surveys) which suggest the same conclusions that one has to wonder how a person regarded with the authority that would justify reviewing manuscripts on eating disorders could be unaware of them.[47]

Moreover, although obesity is not technically part of the accepted diagnostic criteria for an eating disorder, it is worth noting that the Centers for Disease Control and Prevention further states (based on the same *JAMA* study) that "There were 112,000 more deaths than expected in 2000 among obese individuals (BMI of 30 or higher)."[48] If the obesity of these people is a contributing factor in their death, then the underlying cause of their obesity is certainly a contributing factor as well. According to the NIH, 10–15 percent of obese adults have binge eating disorder.[49] It is, therefore, well within the bounds of officially sanctioned statistics to suppose that 10–15 percent of the people whom the CDC says constitute "unexpected" obesity deaths actually die as a result of binge eating disorder; that's 14,000 deaths *per year* from binge eating disorder.[50]

These are the numbers that emerge as a result of a most conservative appropriation of recent and widely accepted research. These numbers reflect an unavoidably incomplete account of deaths attributable to eating disorders, if for no other reason than that we are unable to determine—based on currently available research data—how many people die from bulimia or from "subthreshold" or "partial" eating disorders (EDNOS). Unfortunately, there is no reasonable way to cast doubt on what we have here established, or to argue that it has been somehow inflated or overstated. The grim fact of the matter is this: eating disorders cause a minimum of 30,800 deaths *per year.*

Again, the number needs to be situated for the sake of comparison. In light of our generous efforts to maintain the lowest reasonable estimates while still relying on research acknowledged by the NIMH, it is very likely that more people die annually from eating disorders than from HIV, Parkinson's Disease, homicide, high blood pressure, liver disease, suicide, or septicemia. Based on these conservative numbers, we are able to assert a high probability that *eating disorders are within the top 10 leading causes of death in the United States.*[51]

There are, no doubt, people who consider themselves "experts" in the field of eating disorders research who will scoff at the prevalence and mortality estimates offered in this chapter. At least three such "experts" have already anonymously reviewed this chapter by way of the solicitation of a publisher who was considering picking up this manuscript. While no estimate can be boasted as beyond any possibility of refinement, the bulk of the criticism offered in response to the analysis presented here has not been of the constructive sort one would hope for from people alleging themselves to be interested in improving the condition of the eating disordered.

Despite my consistent effort to remain at the low end of all of the available numbers, every criticism I have received regarding these prevalence and mortality estimates has centered on the allegation that I must, somehow, have inflated the numbers. That there are 27 million people with eating disorders in the United States, and that eating disorders constitute the tenth leading cause of death in the United States, are not claims that current eating disorders orthodoxy is willing to accept. Since the numbers are "too high," the presumption is that there must be some glaring mistakes somewhere in the analysis that has been offered. None of the reviewers thus far, however, has been able to point out any specific problem.

Curiously, not all those who have been kind enough to read this chapter prior to publication have had this same reaction. This chapter has been reviewed by therapists, eating disordered people (in all stages of illness and recovery), researchers, and lay people with no specialized knowledge or experience of eating disorders. The only group to cry foul has been the researchers. That therapists and eating disordered persons would not be surprised by these numbers is to be expected, as they are in positions such that the eating disordered community is already visible; this analysis only serves to confirm the experience of sufferers and therapists alike. People with no specialized knowledge or experience of eating disorders are not able to verify or falsify such estimates; hence, they are accepting this chapter on trust, as they likely would do for any estimate offered to them.

Why are the researchers the ones who resist these claims; 27 million people, tenth leading cause of death? Are the researchers correct? Do we really have numbers here that are inflated beyond any consistency with accepted research? Or does the orthodoxy have something else at stake in trying to caste doubt on a specific prevalence estimate? Is it the case that the researchers who have reviewed this chapter are being cautiously responsible in their hesitancy to acknowledge these prevalence and mortality claims? Or are they attempting to disguise their irresponsibility in not discerning the presence of this epidemic sooner? These questions can be navigated quite easily by setting our estimates side-by-side with the estimates most widely accepted by the nation's leading research institutions.

One of the points previously noted concerning the estimates that have been put forward by research institutions (such as the NIMH and the CDC) is that they offer us a wide range of numbers rather than specific information. We can, however, compare the specific estimates offered here to the range of estimates offered by these institutions and find out whether or not this chapter is within those accepted parameters. And if it is, we can find out if the numbers here are nearer to the low-end, middle, or high-end of that accepted range. Most of the work for such a comparison has already been completed, as it should be recalled that most of the components of our prevalence esti-

Table 1.2.   Eating Disorders Prevalence by Age, Sex, and Diagnosis

Age	Anorexia	Bulimia	Binge Eating Disorder	EDNOS	Totals
			Diagnosis		
10–14	~	1,500,000	~	~	1,500,000
15–19					
F	70,000	120,000	150,000	1,460,000	1,800,000
M	20,000	40,000	90,000	500,000	650,000
Total	90,000	160,000	240,000	1,960,000	2,450,000
20+					
F	2,600,000	3,200,000			
M	300,000	1,200,000			
Total	2,900,000	4,400,000	8,400,000	7,300,000	23,000,000
Totals	2,990,000	6,060,000	8,640,000	9,260,000	26,950,000

mates were derived precisely by adhering to the means of the estimates officially recognized by the NIMH.

Accordingly, the work completed in this chapter can be consolidated into table 1.2 in which the 27 million eating disordered people in the United States are broken down by age, sex, and diagnosis.

We've already noted that the NIMH prevalence estimates for anorexia and bulimia state that: "An estimated 0.5 to 3.7 percent of females suffer from anorexia nervosa in their lifetime. An estimated 1.1 percent to 4.2 percent of females have bulimia nervosa in their lifetime."[52] According to the data from the 2000 census, again previously noted, this gives us a range of 750,000 to 5.3 million anorexic women, and 1.6 million to 6 million bulimic women. This is the officially accepted "expert" opinion. Notice that the total range for anorexic and bulimic women being described by these NIMH numbers is between 2.35 million and 11.3 million. Our total estimate for anorexic and bulimic women is 5.99 million (not including the 10–14 age group, since that group has not been broken down by sex). We are certainly in the middle of the NIMH estimate in this regard.

Also previously noted is the accepted NIMH estimate for binge eating disorder: "[B]etween 2 percent and 5 percent of Americans experience binge-eating disorder."[53] Again, the 2000 census tells us that there are 281 million people in the United States. Thus, the NIMH estimate for binge eating disorder is a range between 5.62 million and 14.05 million persons. Our prevalence estimate for binge eating disorder indicates a total of 8.64 million, which is obviously closer to the low end of the NIMH range.

By process of elimination, the only place where our estimate can possibly be criticized as being inflated is in regard to anorexia and bulimia prevalence among males (which actually makes up a fairly small portion of the overall prevalence figure offered in this analysis), or in regard to EDNOS prevalence. On these points, however, we are not able to say whether or not our estimates are within currently accepted ranges because there are no such prevalence estimate ranges offered by the NIMH or any other recognized research institution.

To put it plainly, the orthodoxy in eating disorders research has nothing to say about how many eating disordered men there are, or about how many people there are with partial (sub-threshold) eating disorders. Asserting that a prevalence estimate is inflated or too high is a comparative claim. But since there are no prevalence estimates that provide a suitable comparison regarding eating disordered males or EDNOS, it is impossible to claim that our estimates here are overstated. The ball is in the court of the critic, so to speak. If researchers truly believe that this estimate is too high, it is their responsibility to provide a better one. That they have made no effort to do so is a fact that needs to be interrogated and explained in some detail, and we will take up this question of silence and ambiguity in the field of eating disorders research in chapter 3.

At every available point of comparison between the estimates provided here and current accepted research, the estimates provided here are consistent with a conservative appropriation of data accepted by the nation's primary research institutions. In light of the noted severity and lethality of eating disorders, both easily demonstrable by way of widely acknowledged and readily available information, our prevalence estimate takes on new significance. We have found that more people suffer from diagnosable eating disorders than any other known illness, and that eating disorders are chronic and deadly to a degree that has few comparisons in the medical field. At this point, we should naturally inquire as to what is being done to remedy this extraordinary epidemic.

NOTES

1. National Eating Disorders Association (NEDA): <http://www.nationaleating disorders.org/>

2. J. Crowther, E. Wolf, and N. Sherwood, "Epidemiology of Bulimia Nervosa," in *The Etiology of Bulimia Nervosa: The Individual and Familial Context,* ed. M. Crowther, D.L. Tennenbaum, S.E. Hobfoll, and M.A.P. Stephens (Washington, D.C.: Taylor & Francis, 1992), 1–26.

C.G.Fairburn, P.J. Hay, and S.L. Welch, "Binge Eating and Bulimia Nervosa: Distribution and Determinants," in C.G. Fairburn & G.T. Wilson, eds., *Binge Eating: Nature, Assessment, and Treatment* (New York: Guilford, 1993), 123–43

R.A. Gordon, *Anorexia and Bulimia: Anatomy of a Social Epidemic* (New York: Blackwell, 1990)

H.W. Hoek, "The Distribution of Eating Disorders," in *Eating Disorders and Obesity: A Comprehensive Handbook,* ed. K.D. Brownell and C.G. Fairburn (New York: Guilford, 1995), 207–11.

C. Shisslak, M. Crago, and L. Estes, "The Spectrum of Eating Disturbances," *International Journal of Eating Disorders* 18, no. 3 (1995): 209–19.

3. Anorexia Nervosa and Related Eating Disorders, Inc. (ANRED). <http://www.anred.com/stats.html> The article cited is M. Makino, K. Tsuboi, and L. Dennerstein, "Prevalence of Eating Disorders: A Comparison Of Western and Non-Western Countries," *Medscape General Medicine* 6, no. 3 (2004).

4. American Psychiatric Association Work Group on Eating Disorders, "Practice Guideline for the Treatment of Patients with Eating Disorders (revision)," *American Journal of Psychiatry* 157, no. 1 (2000): 1S-39S. Cited in NIMH, "Eating Disorders: Facts About Eating Disorders and the Search for Solutions," 2001, NIH Publication No. 01-4901. Available online: <http://www.nimh.nih.gov/publicat/eatingdisorders.cfm#ed1>

5. See "Secondhand Smoke: Questions and Answers," from The National Cancer Institute. <http://www.cancer.gov/cancertopics/factsheet/Tobacco/ETS> This document states that "Approximately 3,000 lung cancer deaths occur each year among adult nonsmokers in the United States as a result of exposure to secondhand smoke."

6. The Somerset & Wessex Eating Disorders Association (England) points out the following: "a diagnosis may vary depending on the system used and also how the range of eating disorders varies between systems. For example someone with bulimic like symptoms may . . . be diagnosed as having: Bulimia Nervosa (ICD-10); Bulimia Nervosa Purging Type (DSM-IV); Bulimia Nervosa Non-Purging Type (DSM-IV); Atypical Bulimia Nervosa (ICD-10); Eating Disorder Not Otherwise Specified (DSM-IV, depending on the frequency and volume of binges); Eating Disorder Unspecified (ICD-10); or Anorexia Nervosa-Binge Eating and Purging Type (DSM-IV, if criteria for anorexia nervosa are also met)." With regard to the Nation Health Service Primary Care Protocols: "It is interesting to note that the Nation Health Service has a number of Primary Care Protocols which can be used for identification of, and referral for, a disorder. Protocol III: is for Eating Disorders (in which only Anorexia Nervosa and Bulimia Nervosa are included)." <http://www.swedauk.org/disorders/definitions.htm>

7. The one notable exception to this is the criteria for diagnosing binge eating disorder. Currently, binge eating disorder is not fully recognized by DSM-IV standards, although many cases will be accommodated by the criteria for "eating disorder not otherwise specified" (EDNOS, 307.50). Moreover, the ICD-10 only provides criteria for "Overeating associated with other psychological disturbances." Noticeably absent from any criteria for the diagnosis of binge eating disorder is the symptom of obesity (or even "morbid" or extreme obesity). This absence indicates, of course, that the vast majority of extremely obese persons are likely to be "normal" eaters. Indeed!

8. It should be noted that this strategy for establishing prevalence statistics is already accepted by the National Institute of Mental Health. Their data concerning the prevalence of anxiety disorders, bipolar disorder and schizophrenia are drawn almost exclusively from two similar studies which cross-referenced smaller amounts of data

with national census information in order to determine the national prevalence estimates for these disorders. Of further interest is the fact that the studies in question, although accorded a principal role in these NIMH statistics, were never published. The
NIMH cites these unpublished works as follows: W.E. Narrow, "One-Year Prevalence
of Depressive Disorders Among Adults 18 and Over in the U.S.: NIMH ECA Prospective Data. Population Estimates Based on U.S. Census Estimated Residential Population Age 18 and Over on July 1, 1998," and W.E. Narrow, "One-Year Prevalence of
Mental Disorders, Excluding Substance Use Disorders, in the U.S.: NIMH ECA
Prospective Data. Population Estimates Based on U.S. Census Estimated Residential
Population Age 18 and Over on July 1, 1998."

9. This information is widely available at the web-site for the United States Census Bureau: <http://www.census.gov/>

10. J. Garry, S. Morrissey, and L. Whetstone, "Substance Use and Weight Loss
Tactics Among Middle School Youth," *International Journal of Eating Disorders* 33,
no. 1 (2002): 55–63.

11. While it could be suggested that this figure is inflated as a result of "experimentation" rather than genuine eating disordered behavior, it should be noted that this
figure is actually quite low as the study from which it is derived made no effort to
identify people who were anorexic or binge eaters. Moreover, the DSM-IV criteria we
are using here suggest no distinction between eating disordered behavior that is attributable to childhood "experimentation" and similar behavior that is not. Vomiting
and laxative use for the purpose of weight management at least supports the likelihood of a diagnosis of bulimia. Since we have no data regarding the number of
anorexics and binge-eaters in this group, our estimate for the 10–14 age group is not
likely to be excessive.

12. E. Kjelsas, C. Bjornstrom, and K. Gotestam, "Prevalence of Eating Disorders
in Female and Male Adolescents (14–15 years)," *Eating Behaviors* 5, no. 1 (2004):
13–25. A preliminary version of this study was also presented at the International Society of Behavioural Medicine's Seventh Annual Meeting in Helsinki—September,
2002.

13. Realistically, these figures do not hold generally for the 15–19 age group. The
reason for thinking this is that we have already noted a significant increase in prevalence among girls just by moving from the 10–14 age group to the youngest end of
the 15–19 age group. It is reasonable to expect that prevalence would continue to increase such that the older people in the 15–19 age group would have a *higher* prevalence of eating disorders than the 15 year olds. But the assumption of consistency will
serve our purposes here, insofar as it will keep us from over-estimating.

It should also be noted that the suggestion that prevalence rates for eating disorders
may be higher in the 15–19 age group than in the 10–14 age group is consistent with
other research which suggests that the average age of onset is between the ages of 14 and
18. See especially I. Attie and J. Brooks-Gunn, "The Development of Eating Regulation
Across the Life Span," in *Developmental Psychopathology—Volume 2: Risk, Disorder,
and Adaptation*, ed. D. Cicchetti and D. Cohen (New York: Wiley, 1995), 332–68.

14. APA Work Group on Eating Disorders, "Practice Guideline."

15. Makino, Tsuboi, and Dennerstein, "Prevalence of Eating Disorders."

16. "[A]n estimated 5 to 15 percent of people with anorexia . . . are male." A.E. Andersen, "Eating Disorders in Males," in *Eating Disorders and Obesity: A Comprehensive Handbook,* ed. K.D. Brownell and C.G. Fairburn (New York: Guilford, 1995), 177–87. This statistic and source cited by the NIMH in "Facts About Eating Disorders."

17. The NIMH mean estimate for anorexia among females, it will be recalled, is 2.1 percent. The female population in 2000 (not including the 10–19 age group) is 122 million. This yields an estimate of 2,562,000.

18. "[B]etween 2 percent and 5 percent of Americans experience binge-eating disorder." R.L. Spitzer, S.Yanovski, T. Wadden, R. Wing, M.D. Marcus, A. Stunkard, M. Devlin, J. Mitchell, D. Hasin, and R.L. Horne, "Binge Eating Disorder: Its Further Validation in a Multisite Study," *International Journal of Eating Disorders* 13, no. 2 (1993): 137–53. This finding also confirmed in B. Bruce, and W.S. Agras, "Binge Eating in Females: A Population-Based Investigation," *International Journal of Eating Disorders* 12 (1992): 365–73. These statistics and sources cited by the NIMH in "Facts About Eating Disorders." The NIH, for example, (according to which 25 percent of American adults are obese) states in "Binge Eating Disorder," NIH Publication No. 04-3589 (2004), that "About 10 to 15 percent of people who are mildly obese and who try to lose weight on their own or through commercial weight-loss programs have binge eating disorder. The disorder is even more common in people who are severely obese." It is, of course, interesting to note that while the NIH openly observes that a significant percentage of obese persons suffer from binge eating disorder, the DSM-IV does not consider obesity to be a diagnostically relevant symptom of disordered eating; see appendix A.

19. S. Banasiak, S. Paxton, and P. Hay, "Evaluating Accessible Treatments for Bulimic Eating Disorders in Primary Care," (research paper presented at University of Melbourne and University of Adelaide, 1998). At the very least, this estimate is intuitively appealing since it tends to be the case that the more severe manifestations of illnesses are attained by progressively fewer people.

20. It will be recalled that within the 10–19 age group we found some 4 million eating disordered people. But the data we used to establish this estimate actually included the EDNOS diagnosis. This age group will, therefore, not be counted again here.

21. The DSM-IV characterizes pica (307.52) as "A pattern of eating non-nutritive substances, lasting for at least a month, such substances as dirt, paper etc." Moreover, "Research suggests that pica occurs in 25–33% of young children and 20% of children seen in mental health clinics." C. Ellis and C. Schnoes, "Eating Disorder: Pica," *eMedicine* (2002). <http://www.emedicine.com/ped/topic1798.htm>. Rumination dis-order (DSM-IV, 307.53) is characterized by "repeated regurgitation and rechewing of food for a period of at least 1 month following a period of normal eating habits."

22. Some might argue that this estimate is ridiculously low as a result of my effort to be conservative, and I would be inclined to agree. The point, however, is not only to be accurate but to sidestep any misgivings that might be expressed by would-be skeptics. It would be stretching the boundaries of responsible research indeed to suggest that our estimations have at any point been excessive, and this is precisely what we are after.

23. Dr. Insel's complete testimony to the House Subcommittee is available online: <http://www.nimh.nih.gov/about/2005budget.pdf>

24. "Alzheimer's disease, the most common cause of dementia among people age 65 and older, affects an estimated 4 million Americans." National Institute of Mental Health, "The Numbers Count: Mental Disorders in America," NIH Publication No. 01-4584 (2001).

25. "Anxiety disorders are serious medical illnesses that affect approximately 19 million American adults." NIMH, "Anxiety Disorders," 1994. "19 million adult Americans ages 18 to 54 have anxiety disorders." National Institute of Mental Health, "Anxiety Disorders Research at the National Institute of Mental Health," 1999, NIH Publication No. 99-4504. Information drawn from Narrow, "One-Year Prevalence of Depressive Disorders."

One of the obvious reasons for the striking prevalence estimate here is that the term "anxiety disorder" is an umbrella term which refers to a multitude of disorders including (but not limited to) Generalized Anxiety Disorder, Obsessive-Compulsive Disorder (OCD), Panic Disorder, Post-Traumatic Stress Disorder (PTSD), Social Phobia (or Social Anxiety Disorder) and Specific Phobias. Although otherwise distinct from one another in their DSM-IV diagnostic criteria, these conditions have the one notable symptom of anxiety in common.

26. "Prevalence estimates range from 2 to 6 per 1,000 children." National Institute of Mental Health, "Autism Spectrum Disorders (Pervasive Developmental Disorders)," 2004, NIH Publication No.04-5511. See also The Autistic Society: <http://www.autisticsociety.org/>, which cites The Southeast Missourian (April 2004) as indicating that there are "1.5 million autistic children and adults."

27. "It [bipolar disorder] affects approximately 2.3 million adult Americans— about 1.2 percent of the population." NIMH, "Going to Extremes: Bipolar Disorder," 2001, NIH Publication No. 01-4595. Information drawn from Narrow, "One-Year Prevalence of Depressive Disorders."

28. "In any given 1-year period, 9.5 percent of the population, or about 18.8 million American adults, suffer from a depressive illness." NIMH, "Depression," 2000, NIH Publication No. 00-3561. Information drawn from L.N. Robins and D.A. Regier, eds., *Psychiatric Disorders in America, The Epidemiologic Catchment Area Study*, (New York: The Free Press, 1990).

29. "In the U.S., approximately 2.2 million adults, or about 1.1 percent of the population age 18 and older in a given year, have schizophrenia." NIMH, "When Someone Has Schizophrenia," 2001, NIH Publication No. 01-4599. Information drawn from Narrow, "One-Year Prevalence of Mental Disorders."

30. American Cancer Society, "Cancer Facts & Figures," 2004. Available online: <http://www.cancer.org/downloads/STT/CAFF_finalPWSecured.pdf>

31. National Institute of Neurological Disorders and Stroke, "Brain Basics: Preventing Stroke," 2004. Available online: <http://www.ninds.nih.gov/disorders/stroke/preventing_stroke.htm> This finding is confirmed by the American Heart Association, "Know the Facts Get the Stats," 2004, according to which: "about 5.4 mil-

lion stroke survivors are alive today." Available online: <http://www.americanheart
.org/presenter.jhtml?identifier=3000996>

32. American Heart Association. "Know the Facts Get the Stats."

33. International Diabetes Federation, "Did You Know?" Available online: <http://
www.idf.org/home/index.cfm?node=37>

34. NIMH, "Facts About Eating Disorders."

35. Recent studies suggest a significant overlap between eating disorders and diabetes, and that this conjunction of illnesses is an exceptional danger. Of interest in this
regard is the recent study of mortality rates for diabetics and anorexics which indicates a mortality rate of 2.2 (per 1,000 person-years) for type 1 diabetes, 7.3 for
anorexia nervosa cases, and 34.6 for concurrent cases. S. Nielsen, C. Emborg, and
A.G. Molbak, "Mortality in Concurrent Type 1 Diabetes and Anorexia Nervosa," *Diabetes Care* 25, no.2 (2002).

36. For more information on the numerous health risks associated with eating disorders, see National Eating Disorders Association, "Health Consequences of Eating
Disorders." Available online: <http://www.nationaleatingdisorders.org>

37. P. Sullivan, "Mortality in Anorexia Nervosa," *American Journal of Psychiatry*
152, (1995): 1073–4.

38. Sullivan achieved somewhat diminished but nonetheless consistent results in a
1998 study which expanded his survey to 49 other published works and direct follow-
up interviews with 70 anorexic patients: P. Sullivan, C. Bulik, J. Fear, and A. Pickering, "Outcome of Anorexia Nervosa: A Case-Control Study," *American Journal of
Psychiatry* 155 (1998): 939–46. That Sullivan's research represents a *minimum* estimate of the mortality rate associated with anorexia was confirmed by several rigorous
and more recent studies. See especially B. Lowe, S. Zipfel, C. Buchholz, Y. Dupont,
D.L. Reas, and W. Herzog, "Long-Term Outcome of Anorexia Nervosa in a Prospective 21-Year Follow-up Study," *Psychological Medecine* 31, (2001): 881–90. "At 21
years follow up, 14 of the 84 patients (17%) had died; 12 due to causes directly related to anorexia nervosa (standard mortality rate 9.8)." In a commentary on Lowe,
et. al., Bulik (co-author of Sullivan's 1998 article) noted that Lowe's findings were
consistent with prior observations. See also L.C. Birmingham, J. Su, J.A. Hlynsky,
E.M. Goldner, and M. Gao, "The Mortality Rate from Anorexia Nervosa," *International Journal of Eating Disorders* 38, no. 2 (2005): 143–6, "The SMR [Standardized
Mortality Rate] for AN [Anorexia Nervosa] was 10.5 . . . Our study confirms the association of anorexia nervosa with a clinically important increase in mortality rate . . . The
strengths of our study are the large sample size [954 patients], [and] the long follow-up period
[20 years]." See also D.L. Reas, E. Kjelsas, T. Heggestad, L. Eriksen, S. Nielsen, F.
Gjertsen,   and   K.G.   Gotestam,   "Characteristics   of   Anorexia   Nervosa-
Related Deaths in Norway (1992–2000): Data from the National Patient Register and
the Causes of Death Register," *International Journal of Eating Disorders* 37, no. 3
(2005): 181–7. This article notes that the mortality rate varies according to the data
from which it is constructed, but the variance is well above Sullivan's accepted 5.6;
the National Patient Register indicates a death rate of 6.46 for anorexia, and the

Causes of Death Register indicates a death rate of 9.93 for anorexia. Also of interest here is that Sullivan's mortality figure is markedly lower than that of the Diabetes Care study (7.3) mentioned above. Not only is Sullivan's work widely accepted, but it appears to be quite conservative in relation to other similar studies.

39. Attie and Brooks-Gunn, "The Development of Eating Regulation."

40. 2.9 million from the population of those over the age of 20 (according to our laborious calculations above), and about 90,000 between the ages of 10 and 19.

41. NIMH, "Facts About Eating Disorders" The statistics presented in this NIMH document are cited as being drawn directly from Sullivan's research.

42. L. Hsu, "Epidemiology of Eating Disorders," *Psychiatric Clinics of North America* 19 (1996): 681–700.

43. K.M. Flegal, B.I. Graubard, D.F. Williamson, and M.H. Gail, "Excess Deaths Associated with Underweight, Overweight and Obesity," *Journal of the American Medical Association* 293 (2005): 1861–7. Cited by the Centers for Disease Control and Prevention in "Efforts to Reduce or Prevent Obesity," available online: <http://www.cdc.gov/od/oc/media/pressrel/fs050419.htm>

44. Flegal, Graubard, Williamson, and Gail, "Excess Deaths Associated with Underweight, Overweight and Obesity."

45. Regrettably, this review was provided anonymously at the request of a prospective publisher for this book—hence, the quote cannot be directly attributed to a specific "expert."

46. Reas, Kjelsas, Heggestad, Eriksen, Nielsen, Gjertsen, and Gotestam, "Characteristics of Anorexia Nervosa-Related Deaths in Norway."

47. See especially P.L. Hewitt, S. Coren, and G.D. Steel, "Death from Anorexia Nervosa: Age Span and Sex Differences," *Aging and Mental Health* 5 (2001): 41–6. Similar age-related mortality rates for anorexia were noted in this study, and the findings were based on a review of some 10 million U.S. death records. Specifically, this study found that 79% of deaths associated with anorexia occurred among individuals older than 45 years, with a median age of 69 years! Other recent publications which corroborate these results include:

- A. Allaz, M. Bernstein, P. Rouget, M. Archinard, and A. Morabia, "Body Weight Preoccupation in Middle-age and Ageing Women: A General Population Survey," *International Journal of Eating Disorders* 23, no. 3 (1998): 287–94.
- D. Beck, R. Casper, and A. Andersen, "Truly Late Onset of Eating Disorders: A Study of 11 Cases Averaging 60 Years of Age at Presentation," *International Journal of Eating Disorders* 20, no. 4 (1996): 389–95.
- L. Hsu and B. Zimmer, "Eating Disorders in Old Age," *International Journal of Eating Disorders* 7, no. 1 (1988): 133–8.
- D. Lewis and F. Cachelin, "Body Image Dissatisfaction and Eating Attitudes in Midlife and Elderly Women," *Eating Disorders: The Journal of Treatment and Prevention* 9, no. 1 (2001): 29–39.
- H.T. Mermelstein and R. Basu, "Can You Ever be Too Old to be Too Thin? Anorexia Nervosa in a 92 Year Old Woman," *International Journal of Eating Disorders* 30, no. 1 (2001): 123–6.

• B.C. Reimann, R.J. McNally, and A. Meier, "Anorexia Nervosa in an Elderly Man," *International Journal of Eating Disorders* 14 (1993): 501–4.

48. CDC, "Efforts to Reduce or Prevenent Obesity."

49. "About 10 to 15 percent of people who are mildly obese and who try to lose weight on their own or through commercial weight-loss programs have binge eating disorder. The disorder is even more common in people who are severely obese." NIMH, "Binge Eating Disorder."

50. It will be recalled that the CDC endorses the claim that 112,000 deaths annually are attributable to obesity. 12.5 percent (the mean of the NIH 10–15 percent claim) of these deaths is 14,000. We have, as well, enough information here to construct a mortality rate for binge eating disorder—since we have estimates for how many people presently suffer from this disease and for how many people die annually. Accordingly, our investigation has shown that there are 8.4 million binge eaters, and that 14,000 of them die annually. That's a mortality rate of approximately 0.16 percent annually, or 1.6 percent per decade. We've already noted that the 5.6 percent per decade mortality rate for anorexia is asserted (by the NIMH) to be "12 times higher than the annual death rate due to all causes of death among females ages 15–24 in the general population" (see note 41 above). The mortality rate for binge eating disorder is nearly one third that of the mortality rate for anorexia. Binge eating disorder, therefore, has a mortality rate 4 times higher than the annual death rate due to all causes of death among females ages 15–24 in the general population, according to the calculations of the NIMH.

I should additionally take great care to point out at this time that I have not argued that binge eating disorder causes an increase in mortality over that of simple obesity. What I have done is to note that the CDC and NIMH assert that a certain portion (10–15%) of obese individuals are obese *because* they suffer from binge eating disorder (and the accuracy of this estimate could certainly be drawn into further question). When the obesity of these people is a contributing factor in their death, therefore, it is obvious that the cause of their obesity is also a contributing factor. Nowhere have I compared, however, mortality rates for binge eating disorder to mortality rates for obesity generally.

51. Our analysis here shows that if even 3,000 people die annually from bulimia and EDNOS *combined*, then eating disorders constitute the 10th leading cause of death in the United States. A searchable database for the leading causes of death, up through the year 2002, is available from the CDC and the National Center for Injury Prevention and Control at this address: <http://webapp.cdc.gov/sasweb/ncipc/leadcaus10.html>. In 2002, the 10th leading cause of death was septicemia at 33,566; suicide was 11th with 31,645; liver disease was 12th with 27,247.

52. APA Work Group on Eating Disorders, "Practice Guideline."

53. R.L. Spitzer, S. Yanovski, T. Wadden, R. Wing, M.D. Marcus, A. Stunkard, M. Devlin, J. Mitchell, D. Hasin, and R.L. Horne, "Binge Eating Disorder: Its Further Validation in a Multisite Study," *International Journal of Eating Disorders* 13, no. 2 (1993): 137–53. This finding also confirmed in Bruce and Agras, "Binge Eating in Females." These statistics and sources cited by the NIMH in "Facts About Eating Disorders."

Chapter Two

Research and Treatment: What Is Being Done?

It should be obvious that in order to remedy something that is very bad, one would at least have to recognize that it was happening and that it was in fact very bad. In the United States, neither of these is the case with respect to disordered eating. By virtue of having drawn figures conservatively from accepted and recent research, this document has provided the first estimate of the prevalence of disordered eating in the United States that is both comprehensive and realistic. If it was not heretofore known how many of us there are, then by default is was not known how many of us were dying or near death as a result of these conditions. The reader is, therefore, cautioned not to expect too much in the way of measures being taken to alleviate the suffering of the eating disordered.

The major player in the funding of eating disorders research is the National Institute of Mental Health. Additionally, the NIMH conducts research on the other mental illnesses previously designated as "serious" and/or "major" by its Director. In order to demonstrate the NIMH's solid commitment to advancing the cause of treatment and prevention for these major illnesses, Dr. Insel—NIMH Director—has fortuitously made information available on his web-site concerning the specific amounts designated for research in the annual NIMH budget.[1] The information presented on the Director's web-site was drawn from fiscal year 2003, the most recent year (at the time of this writing) for which comprehensive figures of this sort have been collected.[2]

Accordingly, table 2.1 shows the 2003 budgeted research dollars for some of the major mental illnesses as disclosed by the NIMH Director. Curiously, neither the Director's page nor the pages of budget documents available online at the NIMH web-site offer any specific information on the funds for eating disorders research.

Table 2.1.   NIMH Research Funds for Major Mental Illnesses

Illness	Research Funds	Portion of Budget
Autism	$51.1 million	3.8 %
Bipolar Disorder	$86.9 million	6.5 %
Major Depression	$212.8 million	15.9 %
Schizophrenia	$311.9 million	23.3 %

There has been a great deal of publicity in the last year concerning an NIMH funded study being conducted at the University of Pittsburgh. This study, which is attempting "to find regions of the human genome that contain genes that influence risk for anorexia" has received a five year commitment from the NIMH at about $2 million per year.[3] Word of this study has been widely circulated, and as a result many of the eating disorders related websites have announcements posted on them soliciting participants for this study.[4] This study, along with the publicity it has received, gives an appearance of affluence to the NIMH eating disorders research budget. A closer examination, however, which pays specific attention to the overall percentage of NIMH research funds devoted to eating disorders, reveals anything but the kind of generous commitment suggested by the funding of the University of Pittsburgh study.

At present, 1.5 percent of the National Institute of Mental Health research budget is directed to eating disorders research.[5] What this boils down to is that the 2003 budget includes $20.1 million in eating disorders research funds.[6] With the exception of the Pittsburgh study, it is unclear to public inquirers exactly how this $20.1 million in eating disorders research funds is being spent. The National Institutes of Health lists past and ongoing clinical trials online by illness, and these available databases include information on the funding source (but not the amount) for each trial.[7] Even a casual perusing of these listings will alert the reader to the fact that institutions other than the NIMH fund research on eating disorders. Most of the non-NIMH funded research is funded by the National Cancer Institute (NCI) and also the National Institute of Diabetes and Digestive and Kidney Diseases (NIDDK). The principal reason why these other organizations conduct eating disorders related research has to do with the well documented relationships that exist between cancer and weight loss (resulting either from the disease itself or from chemotherapy), and between diabetes and weight-related issues. Hence, the interest shown in eating disorders research by the NCI and the NIDDK tends to be tangential at best. Our earlier characterization of the NIMH as the "major player" in eating disorders research funding is, therefore, reasonable and accurate.[8] The skeptic would not, therefore, be able reasonably to claim that the apparently minimal NIMH eating disorders research funds are justified on the grounds that there are sufficient funds elsewhere to take up the slack.

It is revealing indeed to compare this eating disorders research amount to the research amounts (listed above) for other conditions. Since we now have figures for the prevalence of each of these conditions as well as their respective allocated research funds at the NIMH, we can see clearly what the situation looks like. By dividing research dollars by the number of people who suffer from a given condition, a prioritizing of research interests emerges that can only be described as extreme. From the highest priority to the lowest, table 2.2 shows what we find.

Take your time, go back and look at table 2.2 again. Then pick up your jaw from the floor. We have shown, by way of reliable, current, and NIMH accepted research, that eating disorders affect significantly more people than any other known medical condition, and that eating disorders are far more deadly than any of the other illnesses researched by the NIMH. And yet, the prioritizing reflected in the NIMH research budget tells us blatantly that they simply do not care. The other illnesses listed in table 2.2 are bad illnesses, to be sure. At the same time, however, none of these other conditions even has an accepted mortality rate.

How is it that less threatening conditions which are suffered by comparatively few people are researched at $100 per person and beyond, but the per person funds available for researching the most prevalent and deadly "mental illness" ever known would not be sufficient to buy a cup of coffee? Contrast also the hundreds of millions of dollars devoted to the advertising campaign to eliminate secondhand smoke with the research funds available to treat eating disorders, and the priorities are again drawn severely into question; as we've noted already, second hand smoke kills (allegedly) 3,000 people per year while anorexia alone kills nearly 17,000. This is what needs to be called out; this really demands an explanation.

We noted, in the concluding remarks to the previous chapter, that some of the people who occupy positions of authority in the field of eating disorders re-

Table 2.2.   NIMH Per Case Research Funds for Major Mental Illnesses

Illness	NIMH Research Funds	Prevalence	Per Case Funds
Schizophrenia	$311.9 million	2.2 million cases	$141.77
Bipolar Disorder	$86.9 million	2.3 million cases	$37.78
Autism	$51.1 million	1.5 million cases	$34.07
Major Depression	$212.8 million	19 million cases	$11.20
Eating Disorders	$20.1 million	27 million cases	$00.74

search have expressed doubts about our claim that eating disorders affect some 27 million people in the United States. Although the criticism that this specific prevalence estimate is inflated has been shown to be unfounded, it is interesting to note that even in the unlikely circumstance that the critics are correct, it makes little difference with regard to the observation being made here.

Suppose, for the sake of the argument, that the prevalence estimate in the previous chapter is so inflated that it overstates the actual number of eating disordered people tenfold. Even under this ridiculously hyperbolic assumption, the per case research funds for eating disorders are still markedly lower than those for any of the other conditions listed in table 2.2. If there are, for example, only 2.7 million eating disordered people (rather than 27 million)—a number that is far below the very bottom of the estimated prevalence range offered by the NIMH—we still have only $7.44 per case dedicated to eating disorders research. Thus, the appalling situation which comes to light as a result of this analysis cannot be mitigated in the least by trying to fall back on the erroneous assertion that the number of eating disordered people has been overstated.

The extent to which this comparative lack of funding affects the manner in which eating disorders are navigated within the medical community is far reaching indeed. One finds, for example, that there exist no postgraduate training programs that are specifically designed to teach professionals how to treat eating disordered people.[9] Amazingly, there is no other medical condition known currently to afflict humankind of which this could be said. The lack of opportunity for academic specialty is not entirely unexpected, however, given the minimal amount of information that could be generated by a minimal amount of funded research. Put simply, with so little research being funded, specialized academic programs wouldn't be able to develop a sufficient curriculum.

What this means is that (a) the people conducting research have not developed their specialization in the area of eating disorders by way of any specialized accredited academic program, and (b) the meager fruits of these research funds are not utilized in a context specifically designed for their academic application to treatment and further research. The situation, then, is dismal. The funding for research is itself severely anorexic. There are no specialized academic means for training researchers and disseminating their findings. In light of this absence of any specialized accredited academic program, one finds a curiosity which wants to be explained: by precisely what means do people acquire their authoritative status within the field of eating disorders research and orthodoxy?

Let us pause at this point and give voice to the skeptic, for surely our findings here will engender attitudes of disbelief even though we've confined our investigation to information that is quite widely accepted in the medical field. Perhaps (the skeptic might suggest) the current treatment options for eating disorders are highly effective? This might explain the marginalizing of eating disorders in research, since we do not normally find a pressing need for research when we already have the means adequately to treat a particular medical condition. If we are truly adept at treating eating disorders, then the research funds really should be quite small. Here again, however, the skeptic misses the obvious. If there were adequate treatment options, wouldn't there be fewer people dying as a result of disordered eating? In fact, a detailed analysis of most common current treatment practices will show that we are not able to treat disordered eating well at all.

There is, at present, no accepted model or standard protocol for the care and treatment of people with disordered eating. The absence of a sufficient quantity and quality of research data make it difficult to establish a standard protocol for treatment. Although the DSM-IV contains quasi-specific criteria for what constitutes disordered eating, physicians who treat patients with disordered eating have virtually no existing superstructure that is capable of providing guidelines for alleviating the condition. There are, of course, standard guidelines for treating many of the symptoms which result from these conditions; cardiovascular and digestive disorders, malnutrition, teeth with no enamel left on them, complications of the kidneys or liver, high or low blood-pressure, etc. But how to restore a person with disordered eating to a healthy way of life is anyone's guess. Patients, therapists and physicians are left to flounder in a maze of treatment options.

Ranging from the relatively conventional to the truly bizarre, we sufferers have before us a medical buffet which serves as testimony to the guesswork involved in our treatment. The buffet includes such items as psycho therapy, group therapy, drug therapy, art therapy, massage therapy, telephone therapy, animal therapy, yoga, biofeedback, eye movement desensitization and reprocessing (EMDR), gastric by-pass surgery, hypnotism, American Indian "sweat lodges," and every conceivable degree of institutionalization from casual outpatient routines to long-term inpatient regimens which include daily insertion of feeding tubes against patient's wishes while they are under physical restraint.

There are rumors circulating within some of the online eating disorders communities that the genetic research being done on anorexia will eventually be exploited by the diet and weight loss industry, as it is (mistakenly) believed by many people that we could improve the lot of the severely overweight by making them anorexic. Apparently, the only treatment that has yet to be suggested (and I hesitate to include this here out of fear that it may be my only lasting contribution to the field) is the salvaging of material removed from gastric by-pass patients for the purpose of subsequent transplant into anorexics.

The majority of treatments currently in vogue have little or no demonstrated efficacy. To be sure, one indicator of this would be the overall mortality rates for disordered eating. As we've already noted, the mortality rates exceed those of all other mental illnesses many times over. But what about those of us who are survivors?

We might be able to get a more complete picture of treatment efficacy if, along side the telling mortality statistics, we had figures on rates of recovery and relapse. Unfortunately, there is an expected lack of available data in this regard. Information of this sort is what results from responsible efforts to research a medical condition, and we have already shown that no such responsibility is demonstrated with regard to these conditions at the most fundamental levels of research obligation.

At the very least, it would be unreasonable to expect that this investigation could provide a more comprehensive or insightful analysis of the efficacy of eating disorders treatment options than the NIMH itself is willing to fund. The point of this book is not to attempt to squeeze out comprehensive information on treatment options. There are too many different ways to be treated and too little research data on their efficacy in order to accomplish such a task. Our response to the skeptic, therefore, will not be wrapped up in trying to show that there are no effective ways to treat disordered eating. All we need to show in order to make the point here is that actually finding a treatment option that works is little more than a matter of extraordinary good fortune.

On the face of it, it seems absurd that someone would be diagnosed with a life-threatening condition and then find themselves in a situation where there are literally dozens of very different treatment options from which to choose and virtually no means whatsoever by which to tell which ones might have any chance of success. But this is precisely the situation for millions of eating disordered people. We know that we face the very real possibility of death if left untreated, and we know that some people have actually been treated and recovered. At the same time, however, we are aware that what works for one person is often completely ineffective for another. We are thereby forced into a situation of trial and error.

Although this dilemma is frequently acknowledged, the fact that it has resulted from an extreme lack of research data—or that some kind of resolution would be feasible were the NIMH to conduct itself in a medically responsible fashion—is seldom mentioned. The National Association of Anorexia Nervosa and Associated Disorders (ANAD) claims that "There is no one definitive form of therapy recommended for eating disorders," and proceeds to provide a list of some 18 different kinds of therapy currently available.[10] Despite this multitude of options, Anorexia Nervosa and Related Eating Disorders, Inc. (ANRED) adds that "The study of eating disorders is a relatively new field. We have no good information on the long-term recovery process."[11]

The widest range of options in eating disorders treatment is of the outpatient type. It is in this group that we find most therapists, ranging from social workers to psychologists to psychiatrists, as well as clergy and many who have no specialized training whatsoever. Some are excellent and some are charlatans, many are boasting a "new and improved" approach to the treatment of eating disorders. In this group also are the self-help groups, the new-age groups, the hypnotists and ear-staplers, the practitioners of Yoga and Zen and Feng Shui for the kitchen, and so on, *ad infinitum*. To be sure, some (perhaps many) people are helped by treatment approaches of these kinds. But there would be no way to measure the success rate of these approaches to treatment—they are too varied, and many of them are non-professional with no facilities in place to make sure that they follow any accepted procedure or document their outcomes.

Although some people really do benefit from these approaches, attempting to select a treatment plan from these possibilities is little more than a lottery. In our analysis, we will simply have to dismiss some of these approaches as obvious attempts to exploit desperate people who are willing to do nearly anything to find relief from the misery of their condition. At the same time, we must concede that many sufferers actually find relief and recovery though one or more of these treatment options. We are not able, however, to determine the overall efficacy of outpatient treatment in any comprehensive way. We cannot, therefore, justify an absence of research funds on the grounds that we already have effective treatments available in this category, precisely because we don't know the overall efficacy these treatments.

Inpatient treatment is available from a variety of institutions, from hospitals to more specialized treatment facilities. Some specialists claim that inpatient treatment received at privately funded and highly specialized facilities is more effective than treatment received in a more general setting (such as a psychiatric hospital). The principal reason for this seems to be the failure of insurance companies to provide adequate mental health coverage for such hospitalizations. Many insurance companies are severely limiting their coverage of inpatient mental health care even in their "preferred provider" hospitals, covering only 50 percent or less of total costs. The Eating Disorders Coalition (EDC), which is a Washington, D.C. based interdisciplinary group formed "to advance the federal recognition of Eating Disorders as a public health priority" has consistently voiced concerns about the problems caused by lack of adequate mental health benefits from insurance providers, noting the direct relation between inadequate coverage and decreased chances of recovery: "Early discharge before a person has fully recovered from an eating disorder results in a high probability of relapse."[12] In light of the limited financial and temporal framework in which they must provide treatment, it is a wonder that physicians and nurses are able to facilitate as much recovery as they do in psychiatric hospitals. That many people leave these institutions at a healthy weight is testimony to their dedication to heal. At the same time, however, even the most optimistic health care provider is aware that short-term weight maintenance is not a reliable indicator of long-term recovery.

Like many other areas of health care, being able to afford treatment (above and beyond what one's insurance will cover) increases one's chances for a full and lasting recovery. So, how successful are the very best of the voluntary inpatient treatment programs? Here again, we find a tremendous variety of approaches. At present, the most popular profile for one of these private facilities is that they are highly focused in their clientele and treatment approach. Many, for example, only accept females, and some only accept clients in their adolescent years. Faith-based approaches are currently quite popular, as well as programs that are "equine assisted" (that is, the use of horses is incorporated into the program of recovery). Most of these facilities have different levels of treatment available, depending on the needs of their clients. Two of the most well known treatment facilities of this type are the Renfrew Center (with facilities in Connecticut, New Jersey, New York, Pennsylvania, and Florida) and Remuda Ranch (located in Arizona).

Renfrew is considered one of the leading advocates for the treatment of eating disorders in the United States. Their centers accept only female clients, but have no age restrictions. They do not present a faith-based program, and they don't use horses. The first Renfrew facility opened in 1985, and to date some 30,000 women have been treated. Renfrew is one of the few treatment facilities openly to discuss its success rates in an honest fashion. Their website, for example, discloses the results of a study of previous patients three years after discharge from their facilities. The study involved 240 female respondents, and boasts that "former anorexic patients reported an average overall weight gain of 9.4 lbs.," and "25.4% of former bulimic patients reported completely abstaining from bingeing and purging."[13] That's a three year recidivism rate of 75 percent for bulimics. And this is state of the art recovery, the best that money can buy.

Remuda Ranch has only one facility at present. It opened in 1990 and has treated about 6,000 patients since that time. Remuda only treats females, does not have age restrictions, and is a faith-based "equine assisted" program. Remuda has posted some recovery statistics on their web-site that are extraordinary to the point of being suspicious. They claim, among other things, a one year success rate of 92 percent:

> Between 1997 and 2001, Remuda Ranch contacted 705 randomly selected patients at one-year following their discharge from Remuda's inpatient treatment program. Patients received a mailing that contained scientifically-valid and reliable measures of eating disorder symptoms and attitudes. 74% of those contacted responded to our mailing, sufficient to assure valid results. Respondents ranged from 11 to 64 years in age. 92% of respondents no longer met standard (DSM-IV) criteria for an eating disorder.[14]

There are several reasons why careful readers might be suspicious of these numbers. In the first place, conclusions drawn from survey data are usually thought to be "reliable" rather than "valid," since such conclusions are the result of a purely inductive inference. Secondly, the reliability of such a conclusion is in no way insured by the mere size of the sample on which it is based. The important feature of generalizations based on a sample is not so much the size of the sample but whether or not the sample is a fair representation of the population from which it was selected—the size of the sample doesn't tell us whether or not the sample is representative of the population from which it was drawn. Finally, and perhaps most importantly, the ultimate meaning of these statistics is dubious because relatively few of the details of the survey itself have been given. We are not told, for example, whether or not any standardized diagnostic features were incorporated into the questions. Two widely used tools in this regard are the Diagnostic Survey for Eating Disorders (DSED), and the Youth Risk Behavior Survey. One would think that if such a standardized tool had been used to generate this recovery data, saying so would be to Remuda's advantage as it would lend credence to their claim. At the very least, it should be obvious that knowing how many people would meet "standard (DSM-IV) criteria for an eating disorder" after their treatment is only useful if we know also (for the sake of meaningful comparison) how many of them met this criteria *prior* to treatment—but no information in this regard is offered. Nevertheless, our argument here does not turn on the reliability of such survey results.

Recovery statistics not withstanding, facilities such as Renfrew and Remuda do not constitute a realistic option for the vast majority of eating disordered persons due to their expense. These facilities usually attempt to receive JCAHO accreditation, for obvious reasons.[15] Insurance companies are more likely to offer at least some coverage for accredited institutions than for nonaccredited institutions. But the coverage gained by accreditation is simply not enough to off-set the expense for most people. The numbers speak for themselves: Renfrew operates five different facilities, but has only treated 30,000 clients in the past 20 years; Remuda has taken 15 years to treat 6,000 clients in its facility. Keeping in mind that there are 27 million of us in need of some form of treatment, at this rate it would take 1,000 such facilities over 75 years to treat the current population of eating disordered persons.[16]

The overwhelming variety of out-patient treatment options combined with the insurance scuttling and financial inaccessibility of the majority of inpatient treatment options serve to place the person seeking treatment in a casino-type environment. To make things worse, some recent studies strongly suggest that a few of the treatment options that are currently quite popular actually make eating disordered people sicker and more likely to die.

One kind of treatment that one would expect to have a somewhat improved rate of success is involuntary inpatient treatment. It does in fact happen, in cases that are alleged to be "extreme," that an eating disordered person is court ordered to receive inpatient treatment. Since people receiving treatment of this kind are not subject to early discharge based on the dictates of an insurance policy, one would expect them to get a bit farther in the recovery process. This, however, is not the case.

Of interest here is a 1999 study which reported that involuntary commitment of patients with anorexia tended to produce satisfactory short-term results, but lead to an increased mortality rate 5 years after admission to treatment.[17] It will be recalled that the accepted mortality rate for anorexics generally is 5.6 percent per decade.[18] In the 1999 study, however, the authors indicate that mortality more than doubled to 12.7 for anorexics who were involuntarily committed to treatment.[19] This is certainly a finding which merits further investigation.

The explanation for this significantly increased lethality of involuntary inpatient treatment of anorexia is more complex than might initially be suspected. The intuitively obvious explanation would be that involuntary patients have an increased mortality rate because they are sicker (upon admission) than are those who enter similar treatment voluntarily. In fact, this not so, as another study quite plainly demonstrates that involuntary patients are no more or less sick upon entering programs of treatment than are voluntary patients. The relevant research is from 2001, and it includes a detailed analysis of seven years worth of admissions information for voluntary and involuntary anorexic patients at the Eating Disorders Treatment Clinic at the University of Iowa Hospital.[20] In their results, the authors report that: "At admission . . . we found that involuntary patients were similar to voluntary patients in virtually all aspects." They go on to list these "aspects" as including severity of diagnosis, body mass index, mean matched population weight, and performance on a variety of standardized eating disorders surveys.

In the end, the only discernable feature that could be correlated with this increase in mortality was the fact of having entered treatment involuntarily. At the very least, this observation that being involuntary is the only discernable trait that could be at all correlated with such an increase in mortality strongly suggests that coercion has a negative impact on the treatment of anorexia. The results of these two studies—that treating anorexics against their wishes severely increases their mortality, and that anorexics who don't want to be treated aren't really any less healthy than those who seek treatment voluntarily—certainly cast serious suspicion upon the efficacy of compulsory treatment, and also call into question the motives and criteria used for obtaining court orders for such treatment.

This is not the only time that a procedure for treating an eating disorder has been shown to do more harm than good. It has more recently come to light that, at the other end of the eating disorders spectrum, patients who undergo bariatric surgery are at a significantly greater risk because of the procedure itself. There are currently two kinds of bariatric procedures that are most widely performed: adjustable gastric banding, and gastric bypass (sometimes referred to as "Roux-en-Y Gastric Bypass" or RYGB). Adjustable gastric banding involves reducing the size of the opening from the esophagus to the stomach by placing a restrictive band around it, thereby decreasing the amount of food that one could comfortably eat within a fixed time. Gastric bypass surgery is more invasive as it involves a permanent reduction in stomach size by actually bypassing most of the stomach and connecting the esophagus directly to the small intestine. The result of gastric bypass surgery is, of course, supposed to be similar to that of adjustable gastric banding in that the patient's capacity to ingest food within a fixed time is reduced. Of these two bariatric procedures, gastric bypass surgery is by far the most popular, making up 80 to 90 percent of all bariatric procedures currently performed.[21]

While the gastric bypass procedure is alleged to be a treatment for obesity, whether or not this is in fact so is open to some question. An article which recently appeared in the *Journal of the American Medical Association* states that "as little as 0.6% of patients who qualify for bariatric surgery undergo a bariatric surgical procedure."[22] This minimal participation in bariatric procedures by obese patients is even more curious when one takes note of the fact that the estimated number of such surgeries being performed each year has increased tenfold between 1998 and 2005.[23] Why there would be such an increase in these procedures and yet such minimal participation in their alleged benefits by obese patients is a question that will receive further investigation in subsequent chapters.

By virtue of what these procedures intend to accomplish—a reduced capacity to ingest food—they have all the appearance of attempting to treat binge eating disorder more directly than obesity. As a treatment for binge eating disorder, however, gastric bypass surgery would have to be understood as a failure as it has actually been shown to be a significant contributor to the development of anorexia and bulimia. The results of a study published in 2002 state clearly that:

People suffering from morbid obesity risk developing anorexic and bulimic symptoms as a consequence of the restrictions in eating behavior or during the period of weight loss that follows gastric surgery.[24]

If gastric bypass surgery is a treatment for obesity, then it is a failure since it appears to be largely unavailable to the vast majority of obese patients. If, on the other hand, the procedure is supposed to treat binge eating disorder, then it is a failure as well since it is known to precipitate the development of other forms of disordered eating. The medical community seems uncertain at best regarding the overall efficacy of gastric bypass surgery. It has been asserted in another recent (*JAMA*) article that efficacy is in fact impossible to determine given (a) the wide variation in the ways in which this procedure is performed and conjoined with other interventions such as weight loss programs, and (b) that establishing control groups for randomized trials is considered unethical when some of the patients under consideration might be qualified for the procedure and actually want (or need) the procedure, but could conceivably be denied the procedure by way of selection into the control group.[25] Moreover, we are not able to compare mortality statistics for those undergoing this procedure with mortality statistics for the population of obese persons generally, if for no other reason than that we don't know what the mortality rate is for simple obesity. Whether or not gastric bypass surgery helps people is a question that (according to authorities considered best equipped to provide us with an answer) can't actually be answered.

The undemonstrated efficacy of a procedure the use of which is growing at such a rapid pace constitutes sufficient reason for caution. Moreover, it is a recently established fact that the rate of hospitalization for people who have this procedure is twice as high after surgery as it is prior, with nearly all rehospitalizations being procedure related.

The cumulative admission rate for the 3-year period prior to RYGB was 20.2% compared with the cumulative 3-year admission rate after RYGB of 40.4% . . . the current study demonstrates that the rates of hospitalization double in the years after operation and that many of these admissions are directly attributable to this procedure.[26]

The consensus of those regarded as experts in the field of bariatrics speaks for itself. According to currently accepted research and published studies, the efficacy of this procedure cannot be determined, patients display an increased risk of anorexia and bulimia after surgery, and patients are hospitalized twice as much after the surgery as they were before. That these same experts would continue to tell us that the benefits of bariatric procedures outweigh the risks despite their very clear (and somewhat euphemistic) admission that "there is a gap between the proliferation of these procedures and the evidence base needed to understand key components in their use" is a curiosity which wants to be explained.[27]

The big picture with regard to the treatment of eating disorders is itself quite disordered. There are more treatment options available than one could detail in a book of this size. There is at present no one form of treatment that the medical community is willing to adopt as a standard model for any form of disordered eating. Most of the outpatient treatments and bariatric procedures currently available are unregulated and require no specialized training. There is recognized research which suggests that some widely practiced treatments for eating disorders, far from making people better, actually double a person's chances of dying as a result of their condition; and some treatments that are supposed to mitigate the symptoms of one eating disorder are now thought in fact to cause other eating disorders and make people twice likely to be hospitalized. This is an intolerable situation for those of us with disordered eating. It is also intolerable for our families who watch us try to recover amidst this ocean of ambiguity and unseen danger. At the very least, it would be absurd indeed to try to justify the appalling lack of research by drawing attention to the treatments that are currently available.

The Centers for Disease Control and Prevention has issued a statement on obesity which summarizes the overall approach to treating disordered eating in the United States. The current CDC statement reads as follows:

> Genetics and the environment may increase the risk of personal weight gain. However, the choices a person makes in eating and physical activity also contributes to overweight and obesity. Behavior can increase a person's risk for gaining weight . . . weight gain is a result of extra calorie consumption, decreasing calories used (physical activity) or both. Personal choices concerning calorie consumption and physical activity can lead to energy imbalance . . . Overweight and obesity result from an energy imbalance. This involves eating too many calories and not getting enough physical activity.[28]

In other words, the best advice that the primary health agencies can give at this time concerning disordered eating is simply to make better "choices" in what one eats. One wonders, if the principal cause of my disordered eating is my having made bad choices, then why is the NIMH funding genetic research? Why even include eating disorders in the DSM-IV at all? That's what 1.5 percent of the research budget gets us, that's what is being done.

Physicians and psychiatrists justify the most painful and the least efficient (and even harmful) forms of treatment by noting that the conditions being treated are serious and, if left untreated, could result in permanent bodily damage or even death. While this is certainly an accurate statement about disordered eating, it by no means justifies any and every possible way of treating our conditions. With regard to all forms of medical treatment, the relevant question has not so much to do with the perceived severity of the condition being treated as it has to do with whether or not the treatment will provide any real improvement in a person's health. To be sure, many people do not survive an eating disorder. But if the current treatments being offered are accessible only to a miniscule minority, or if they do not improve our chances for survival (or if they actually decrease our chances of survival), then we need to rethink our strategies and long-term goals for alleviating this form of suffering.

Some people will surely read too much into these remarks and misconstrue them as advocating an absence of treatment for disordered eating. But this would be a precarious inference indeed; that the inadequacies of current treatments somehow demonstrate that there should be no treatments at all. In point of fact, if anyone advocates an absence of treatment for these conditions, it is the National Institute of Mental Health, which does so by placing this most prevalent of all known medical conditions in last place in terms of research priorities.

For some of us, good fortune combines with well qualified loving health care providers and we get better—but we have shown that this is not the norm. Those of us who are long-term survivors of disordered eating are a very small minority indeed. The relevant and pressing questions, then, are: Why is recovery not the norm? and: What should we do differently?

NOTES

1. Dr. Insel's NIMH web-site: <http://www.nimh.nih.gov/about/director.cfm> The information presented here appeared on the NIMH Director's web-site in the fall of 2004 and remained online through the spring of 2005.

2. The total NIMH budget for FY 2003 was $1,339,283,000. For more detailed information about the NIMH annual budgets for recent years, the reader is encouraged to consult the online documents made public through the NIMH web-site at this address: <http://www.nimh.nih.gov/about/budget.cfm>

3. "The National Institute of Mental Health-funded study is a five-year grant, with more than $10 million in funding, which brings together 11 groups of researchers from North America and Europe (10 clinical centers and one to analyze data) to find regions of the human genome that contain genes that influence risk for anorexia."

University of Pittsburgh Press Release. <http://www.wpic.pitt.edu/research/angenetics/ press_release.html>

4. See, for example, <http://www.something-fishy.org/> The following solicitation was posted on the *Something Fishy* "special bulletin" section on November 23, 2004: National Institute of Mental Health—International study seeks to determine whether a gene might predispose individuals to develop anorexia nervosa. Investigators need families with at least two members who have or had anorexia nervosa and who would be willing to participate. The study involves the completion of interviews, questionnaires and a blood draw. For additional information call [# omitted].

5. This statistic is for the FY 2004 NIMH budget. The 1.5% figure was obtained directly from the NIMH at my request. Also noted in their correspondence with me was the fact that eating disorders research funding has grown from a previous share of 1% of the budget in 1994—a 50% increase over the last 10 years. In order to insure the accuracy of this figure, several other knowledgeable sources were asked to confirm it. Dr. Patrick Sullivan (who's work on mortality rates in anorexia is referenced in the previous chapter, and whose work is endorsed and has been funded by the NIMH) was able to confirm this figure in personal correspondence, as was the Harvard Eating Disorders Center (HEDC) <http://www.hedc.org/>

6. We're extrapolating somewhat here, but in a generous way. The 1.5% figure reflects the research funds from the FY 2004 NIMH budget. Since the research funds for the other illnesses mentioned above have not yet been similarly collected and made available, we're using the 2003 budgetary figures for our comparison—assuming that the 1.5% for eating disorders research applied to 2003 as well. In fact, the 2003 budget probably included less than 1.5% for eating disorders research (since, according to the NIMH, there has been recent growth in the eating disorders portion of the budget). Moreover, the other illnesses have been growing in research funds at a considerably faster pace than eating disorders; in the last 4 years alone, increases for all the other conditions mentioned have ranged from 50% (bipolar disorder) to 165% (autism). Hence, the 1.5% figure's application to the 2003 budget represents a "best possible" scenario for that year. 1.5% of $1,339,283,000 is $20,089,245.

7. A searchable database appears at this address: <http://clinicaltrials.gov/>. The NIH also makes available online information about past research grants and funding awards (at least back to 1972) on its CRISP web-site (CRISP: Computer Retreival of Information on Scientific Projects). CRISP is also a searchable database, and it does not include information on specific dollar amounts: <http://crisp.cit.nih.gov/crisp/ crisp_query.generate_screen>

8. The primacy of the NIMH's role in research funding for eating disorders was also confirmed (in personal correspondence) by Dr. Patrick Sullivan.

9. This also according to the Harvard Eating Disorders Center, <http://www .hedc.org/>

10. ANAD: <http://www.anad.org/site/anadweb/content.php?type=1&id=6901>

11. ADRED: <http://www.anred.com/stats.html>

12. EDC: <http://www.eatingdisorderscoalition.org/reports/policyrecs.html>

13. Treatment outcome statistics are readily available on the Renfrew web-site: <http://www.renfrew.org/treatment-outcomes.asp>. For corroboration, see D. Gleaves,

G. Post, K. Eberenz, and W. Davis, "A Report of 497 Women Hospitalized for the Treatment of Bulimia Nervosa," *Eating Disorders: The Journal of Treatment and Prevention* 1 (1993): 134–46. This study analyzed pretreatment, posttreatment, and 1-, 2-, and 3-year follow-up data on bulimia nervosa inpatients who were admitted to treatment programs over a 4-year period. It is noted in the results that 25% of the women reported being completely abstinent from bingeing and purging, while the remainder continued to display sub-threshold (EDNOS) bulimic symptoms.

14. <http://www.remuda-ranch.com/about_us/outcome.asp>

15. JCAHO—Joint Commission of Accreditation of Healthcare Organizations. <http://www.jcaho.org/>

16. Between Renfrew and Remuda, we find that one facility treats about 350 clients per year. 1,000 facilities, then, could treat 350,000 clients in a year. 27 million divided by 350,000 is about 77 years, so it's not just hyperbole. Moreover, in the unlikely event that our prevalence estimate is overstated even as much as tenfold, it would still take 100 of these facilities 75+ years to treat all of us with disordered eating!

17. R. Ramsay, A. Ward, J. Treasure, and G.F. Russell, "Compulsory Treatment in Anorexia Nervosa. Short-Term Benefits and Long-Term Mortality," *British Journal of Psychiatry* 175 (1999): 147–53.

18. P. Sullivan, "Mortality in Anorexia Nervosa," *American Journal of Psychiatry* 152, (1995): 1073–4.

19. While this mortality rate for involuntary patients is twice that of Sullivan's accepted mortality rate for anorexics *generally*, it is important to note that the authors of this study further distinguished mortality rates for involuntary patients from mortality rates for voluntary patients. In this study, voluntary patients' mortality rate was only 2.6. Thus, involuntary treatment has a mortality rate *five times* that of voluntary treatment, according to this study.

20. T. Watson, W. Bowers, and A. Andersen, "Involuntary Treatment of Patients with Eating Disorders," *Eating Disorders Review* 12, no. 2 (2001).

21. H.P. Santry, D.L. Gillen, and D.S. Lauderdale, "Trends in Bariatric Surgical Procedures," *Journal of the American Medical Association* 294, no. 15 (2005); 1909–17. "Gastric bypass was the most commonly performed bariatric surgical procedure, accounting for 80% to 90% of all procedures during the study period [2002]."

22. B.M. Wolfe and J.M. Morton, "Weighing in on Bariatric Surgery," *Journal of the American Medical Association* 294, no. 15 (2005): 1960–3.

23. "The estimated number of bariatric surgical procedures increased from 13,365 in 1998 70 72,177 in 2002 . . . if our observed rate of growth continues, there will be approximately 130,000 bariatric procedures in 2005 and as many as 218,000 in 2010." Santry, Gillen, and Lauderdale, "Trends in Bariatric Surgical Procedures."

24. J.A. Guisado, F.J. Vaz, J.J. Lopez-Ibor, M.I. Lopez-Ibor, J. del Rio, and M.A. Rubio, "Gastric Surgery and Restraint from Food as Triggering Factors of Eating Disorders in Morbid Obesity," *International Journal of Eating Disorders* 31 (2002): 97–100.

25. "Perhaps the most important barrier to effective bariatric surgical research has been the absence of an adequate control group . . . many surgeons believe that genuine

clinical equipoise does not exist between operative and non-operative options and therefore consider randomization to be unethical . . . competing surgical interventions suggest that . . . generalizability of these results is limited due to the lack of standardization in technical components that define the different types of bariatric procedures and the way that these procedures are described . . . Another important limit to generalizability is that bariatric procedures often achieve weight loss through perioperative behavioral interventions, including presurgical education, active support groups, other multidisciplinary activities, and close follow-up. These additional interventions are inconsistently reported and only occasionally critically evaluated. As a result, it is unclear how these interventions contribute to weight-loss success . . ." A.P. Courcoulas and D.R. Flum, "Filling the Gaps in Bariatric Surgical Research," *Journal of the American Medical Association* 294, no. 15 (2005): 1957–60.

26. D.S. Zingmond, M.L. McGory, and C.Y. Ko, "Hospitalization Before and After Gastric Bypass Surgery," *Journal of the American Medical Association* 294, no. 15 (2005): 1918–24.

27. Courcoulas and Flum, "Filling the Gaps in Bariatric Surgical Research."

28. Centers For Disease Control and Prevention, "Overweight and Obesity: Contributing Factors," 2005. Available online: <http://www.cdc.gov/nccdphp/dnpa/obesity/contributing_factors.htm>

Chapter Three

Manifesto: Why We Have to Come Out

The scenario that has come to light so far goes something like this. Since the prevalence of disordered eating is largely unacknowledged, seeking the means by which to facilitate our recovery is not a primary concern for very many people. This fact is evidenced in the NIMH research budget and, as we discussed in the previous chapter, directly influences what sorts of treatment options become available to us. These are direct cause and effect links in the chain of facts. We are not recognized as being among those in need of medical assistance. We are not counted out loud, only with vague estimates so as to skirt the issue of our epidemic. Therefore, our conditions are not researched. Therefore, the treatments we are offered do not work. As a result of this systematic exclusion from the benefits of adequate health care, we die in huge numbers; eating disorders are within the top 10 leading causes of death in the United States. The organizations responsible for our inclusion in the health care arena know this as they are familiar with the currently accepted research from which these conclusions follow, but the best they have to offer is a lottery of treatment options, some alleged "nutritional information" that will help us make wiser choices about what we eat, and court ordered feeding tubes and restraints just in case we don't take their advice. It is as though someone were trying to solve the nation's eating disorders epidemic with the "just say no" strategy that failed miserably to curb illegal drug use in the 1980s.

One example of the extraordinarily duplicitous attitude advanced by government research institutions is that of the Centers for Disease Control and Prevention. Among the more revealing statements recently issued by the CDC are the ones addressing mortality rates in obesity. Late in 2004, the CDC claimed that obesity would become a more prevalent cause of death than smoking in the near future, with deaths caused by obesity predicted to reach the 400,000 mark annually within the next few years. Then, a month or so later, in January of 2005, the CDC issued a revision to this statement, saying that a calculation error had been made, that obesity deaths would not overtake tobacco deaths after all, and that only 300,000 people were going to die of obesity per year. Amazingly, in April of 2005, the CDC backed off yet again, suggesting that the 300,000 estimate was at least 15 times too high. At present, no specific obesity mortality estimate is forthcoming from the CDC. Rather, some statistics from a study recently published in the *Journal of the American Medical Association* are quoted on the CDC web-site and their interpretation is left to the reader.

> There were 112,000 more deaths than expected in 2000 among obese individuals (BMI of 30 or higher). Underweight individuals (BMI of less than 18.5) had a higher risk of death with nearly 34,000 more deaths than expected. Being overweight (BMI of 25–29.9) was not associated with excess mortality. The study found that 87,000 fewer deaths than expected were associated with being overweight.[1]

The attitude implied by these revisions is that the public should be relieved that obesity isn't near the problem we initially believed. There is certainly evidence which is inconsistent with the CDC's portrayal of obesity as less alarming than previously thought. According to Keith Davis, for example, owner of the Goliath Casket Company—the oldest oversized coffin company in the United States—casket companies nationally are selling 200–300 times more oversized coffins today than they were just 15 years ago. It would be difficult indeed to postulate some cause for this increase in sales of oversized caskets that did not involve a corresponding increase in deaths of oversized people.[2]

Counterevidence by itself, however, doesn't quite reveal the duplicity which we have in mind here. In addressing the CDC's apparent lack of alarm over the growing problem of obesity, it is helpful to remember that obesity is not considered by experts to be a diagnostically reliable indicator of disordered eating; nowhere in the diagnostic criteria for any eating disorder is obesity mentioned. And herein lies the duplicity. The advice given by the CDC as a remedy to obesity is to adjust the way that we eat:

> Personal choices concerning calorie consumption and physical activity can lead to energy imbalance . . . Overweight and obesity result from an energy imbalance. This involves eating too many calories and not getting enough physical activity.[3]

If obesity is not taken to be an indicator of disordered eating, then why correct the problem of obesity by adjusting the way that we eat? On the other hand, if obesity can be addressed by eating differently, then obesity really does indicate eating problems, doesn't it? But obesity cannot be both absent from the diagnostic criteria for disordered eating *and* remedied by changing people's eating habits. That's duplicity.

Want some more? In a strange coincidence, the same day (19 April 2005) that the CDC offered its latest comforting "revision" on obesity mortality rates, the United States Department of Agriculture unveiled its revised version of the "food pyramid."[4] Although the new food pyramid (now referred to as "MyPyramid") outlines the same basic food groups as the old pyramid, it appears turned on its side so that the food groups are no longer arranged hierarchically. The USDA, which oversees the Dietary Guidelines Advisory Committee in conjunction with Health and Human Services, offered two main reasons for its revised food pyramid. First, the new MyPyramid is supposed to be a bit simpler to understand. Whether or not this is so is certainly debatable, however, as the USDA's web-site for MyPyramid explicitly states that:

> The content of this website is not appropriate for use in the development of authoritative statements, as provided for in the Food and Drug Administration Modernization Act. This content has been developed based on the Dietary Guidelines for Americans, 2005, which has the potential to provide authoritative statements. Only statements included in the Executive Summary and Key Recommendations boxes of the Dietary Guidelines can be used for identification of authoritative statements.[5]

In other words, the material on the official USDA MyPyramid web-site is extrapolated from the *Dietary Guidelines* (the government document produced by the Dietary Guidelines Advisory Committee) such that the USDA will not commit itself to what MyPyramid suggests. For "authoritative statements" we are referred to the original document itself. It is not clear, however, to what extent (if at all) the 2005 *Dietary Guidelines* will be helpful to the general public. The *Dietary Guidelines* makes clear its intent in noting that it "is intended primarily for use by policy makers, healthcare providers, nutritionists, and nutrition educators."[6] Moreover, the *Dietary Guidelines* appears to have a comical view of the intelligence of the policymakers and healthcare providers for whom it is written, as the document further states that "A basic premise of the *Dietary Guidelines* is that nutrient needs should be met primarily through consuming foods."[7]

The *Dietary Guidelines* took nearly two years to produce. Nowhere in this 80 page document, however, which is filled with charts, graphs, and technical medical terminology, is there even a single statement indicating the detrimental effects of fast food, or junk food, or sugar.[8] This is the document which is intended to enable Americans to make the informed food choices alluded to by the CDC, but it contains literally no information about the foods that are most likely to precipitate the condition of obesity. So much for simplifying.

The second reason offered for the new MyPyramid was that the original food pyramid wasn't working well enough. According to Agriculture Secretary Mike Johanns "Many Americans can dramatically improve their overall health by making modest improvements to their diets and by incorporating regular physical activity into their daily lives."[9] One has to wonder if the Agriculture Secretary would have done well at least to touch base with the CDC before making such a statement. Indeed, on the same day that the CDC told us that the obesity problem is a mere fraction of what we formerly believed, the USDA revised the official guideline for eating precisely because it had been a failure in preventing obesity.

Which government agency are we to take seriously here? The CDC says that obesity isn't as much of a problem as previously thought, and the USDA says that efforts to prevent obesity have failed; the CDC insists that we make better food choices, and the USDA mentions nothing about obviously problematic foods in its guidelines. That's duplicity.

Those of us with disordered eating are the victims of wide-spread and systematic discrimination. Eating disordered readers will not find this claim at all surprising, normal eaters will probably have the urge to skip this chapter thinking that the author is surely overstating the situation. The principal basis for this claim, however, has already been uncovered in previous chapters—we just need to call it what it really is and look more closely at its sources and its devastating effects. The NIMH—the primary research institution for mental illnesses in the United States—allocates nearly 200 times more research funds per patient for schizophrenia than for eating disorders. This, even though there are 14 times more eating disordered people than there are schizophrenics, and even though many thousands of people die from eating disorders while schizophrenia has a mortality rate of zero.[10] The NIMH allocates 51 times more research funds per patient for bipolar disorder than for eating disorders. This, even though there are 14 times more eating disordered persons than there are people suffering from bipolar disorder (another mental illness with a mortality rate of zero).[11] Per patient research funds for autism are 46 times greater than for eating disorders; there are 18 times more eating disordered people than there are autistic people and no specific mortality rate has been established for autism.[12] "Discrimination" is a word we use when an inequity is unjust, and there is no justification for a distribution of research funds that is so outstanding in its excess for some and at the same time its lack for others.

Unquestionably, all of these conditions merit significant research. But whatever criteria are the means by which we establish that this is so (prevalence, mortality, etc.), eating disorders merit more research than these other conditions. At the top-level of decision-making with regard to research, classification of diseases, and recommended treatments, we constitute an oppressed group. Eating disorders are classified as illnesses in the DSM-IV, but in a manner that is ambiguous and often inconsistent with other diagnostic manuals. Eating disorders are minimally researched, so minimally in fact that there is no accepted model for treating any of these conditions. The advice of the CDC serves to make those of us who suffer responsible for our own care with little more than the suggestion that we need to make better choices. No other known "illness" is treated in such an irresponsible manner.

Why does "top-level decision-making" (i.e., NIH, NIMH, CDC, USDA) operate in this fashion? If there is no rational medical explanation for such inequity, then why the inequity? The simple answer, unfortunately, is money. To put it plainly, the NIMH has shown a consistent willingness to put aside research that is merited on medical grounds and give preference to research that will result in marketable pharmaceuticals. Schizophrenia, bipolar disorder, and depression, are the most expensively researched illnesses at the NIMH, and they are also the conditions over which pharmaceutical companies are most aggressively competing for marketable treatment options. The fact that these illnesses lend themselves to conventional prescription drug models of treatment is perhaps advantageous to those who suffer their effects, but it is also disadvantageous to those of us who suffer from other conditions that are not readily treated in this way. Evidently, there is so much market potential in prescription drug treatments for some mental illnesses, that it is not worthwhile to research those that do not fit this model.

Pharmaceutical companies have certainly explored the possibility of treating disordered eating with prescription drugs, most notably antidepressants. These prescriptions have been found to be somewhat successful in alleviating symptoms for anorexic and bulimic patients. Wide-spread use of antidepressants for these disorders, however, is untenable as these drugs are inconsistently efficacious and often have the side effect of weight gain which, in many cases, dissuades the eating disordered person from compliant use.

Recent marketing reports conducted by and for pharmaceutical companies have evidenced a frustrated and cold attitude toward sufferers of disordered eating, often noting the conjunction of the potential demand for effective drugs and the difficulty successfully of developing them. It is interesting to note that marketing reports for pharmaceutical companies are printed in very limited supply and rarely made available for review or purchase by the general public. When supplies and policy permit public sale of these documents, the prices are prohibitive—ranging from hundreds to thousands of dollars per copy. The impression one gets, of course, is that public readership is unwanted.

One such marketing report reads like a USDA manual for the processing and distribution of meat. Bearing the title "Opportunities In Obesity, Anorexia, and Bulimia," the document includes chapters on:

- "Measurement of Skinfold Thicknesses"
- "Grading Obesity"
- "Summary of Animal Models of Obesity Caused by Diet, Chemicals, and Surgery"
- "Market Potential in Anorexic States and Bulimia"
- "Direct Carcass Analysis."[13]

Reference to the bodies of the eating disordered as "carcasses" is about as dehumanizing as it gets. One wonders if the pharmaceutical attitude isn't at least as disordered as that of the anorexic or bulimic or binge eater.

Had this book been written several years earlier, of course, the very suggestion that some NIMH researchers would be willing to let medical concerns take a back seat to the financial concerns of pharmaceutical corporations would have been laughed at as a wild conspiracy theory. We know now, however—after the story was brought to light by the Los Angeles Times in 2003, and after a year's worth of Congressional hearings in 2004, and after the unveiling of new ethics rules for NIH employees in 2005—that the hands of the pharmaceutical companies have extended, perhaps more deeply than we might have imagined, into the pockets of government researchers and scientists for a very long time. According to the numerous reports still being printed in the nation's largest newspapers, all of the organizations which make up the National Institutes of Health (including the NIMH), have been affected by this "scandal." The Los Angeles Times has reported that more than 500 NIH scientists have been receiving money from drug companies while at the same time researching drugs made by these companies for possible FDA approval. Moreover, these researchers have rarely indicated to their subjects the full nature of their relationships with the companies who will potentially profit from future manufacture and sale of the trial drugs. All of this has been confirmed in a lengthy series of congressional investigations during most of 2004, resulting in some new conflict of interest policies for NIH researchers (the congressional hearings have not, however, resulted in any disciplinary action whatsoever). The new policies, recently unveiled by NIH Director Dr. Elias A. Zerhouni, are supposed to facilitate a new trust in the NIH. In its continuing coverage of this story, the Los Angeles Times recently published an article which includes the following information:

The 2003 reports, along with articles published by The [Los Angeles] Times last year, raised questions about NIH scientists' impartiality in overseeing clinical trials and in making recommendations to doctors for treating patients. The articles were cited by congressional leaders in their requests to Zerhouni a year ago for documentation of the drug industry payments to NIH scientists. Those and other records reviewed recently by The Times identified at least 530 NIH scientists who accepted fees, stock or stock options from biomedical companies from 1999 through 2003 . . . Referring to the pervasive intermingling of pharmaceutical marketing with medical research nationally, Zerhouni said the time had come for the NIH to provide "at least one source of public health information in the country that can be completely trusted. We believe that we need to hold NIH and ourselves as scientists at NIH to a higher standard, because we do have national public health responsibilities," he told a news conference at the agency's headquarters . . . For the better part of the last year, the NIH director had fought against imposing an across-the-board ban on industry consulting.[14]

The details of this situation are readily available as articles such as the above are, at the time of this writing, being picked up by much of the nation's news media. Our point here is not to re-hash what has been in the news for the last year or so, but rather to take it up in the context of our assessment of the current state of eating disorders research and treatment. It is obvious enough that the medical justification for the NIMH refusal to research our conditions is wanting. The explanation for the lack of research and resulting lack of accepted models of treatment for disordered eating is financial; *our deaths are permissible because our carcasses are not profitable.*

NIH scientists are no longer allowed to accept "consulting fees" from outside organizations "(biotechnology, pharmaceutical, medical device companies, and others with similar interests)."[15] While this new policy is subject to revision under the auspices of Health and Human Services, it is unclear whether or not this policy will result in a tangible improvement in research practices at NIH member organizations. Not only was the NIH Director fiercely reluctant to impose such a policy (as noted in the LA Times article above), but the "ban" on these lucrative financial arrangements has expectedly been met with a less than enthusiastic attitude by many of the affected NIH scientists. A recent article in the Washington Post, for example, offered the following details on a notably unfriendly dialogue between the NIH Director and NIH employees:

National Institutes of Health director Elias Zerhouni stood before hundreds of NIH employees Wednesday to explain why it had become necessary for him to impose, in his words, "drastic" restrictions on stock ownership and other forms of outside income, which took effect yesterday for agency employees. "What

I'm asking you to do is hold your fire until you hear the details," he told the crowd assembled in an auditorium on the agency's campus in suburban Bethesda, Md. They held. And when he was done, they let him have it. One after another, scientists, doctors and other agency staffers stepped up to the microphones and raged against the new rules, made public on Tuesday. By the time it was over, 90 minutes later, nary a positive word had been uttered about the new policy.[16]

This lack of willingness to reform research practices was more explicitly addressed by Irving Kent Loh, M.D. in an editorial letter in the LA Times. Dr. Loh states:

> Private industry may now begin to pick off the best and brightest with promises of fully funded laboratories and excellent compensation. The problem will be that their research will be targeted to produce products and not the basic research that leads to fundamental breakthroughs.[17]

Dr. Loh's observation is an important one, as it draws attention to the fact that the reforms currently being sought in the NIH will simply recreate externally the situation that they seek to remedy internally. The problem is that "product" has always been of primary importance, and it still will be. Despite these belated attempts at reform, the bodies of the eating disordered will remain at the status of carcass.

The financial considerations that have been operating in the background of medical research have severely impacted people with disordered eating. We see this at work in specific connection with research relating to anorexia and bulimia—such research is almost non-existent as it is less profitable than research into other conditions. Similar financial considerations offer themselves in an explanatory fashion regarding the continued performing of gastric bypass surgery. As we noted in the previous chapter, gastric bypass surgery has not been demonstrated to be the least bit effective in alleviating obesity, especially as it relates to overeating. This procedure has, however, been shown to increase one's risk of developing anorexia and bulimia.[18] It is also the case that one is twice as likely to be hospitalized after this surgery than before, precisely because of complications resulting from the surgery itself.[19] Why, in light of these published observations, is the performing of this surgery increasing at such a rapid pace? Money plays a significant role in answering this question, suggesting that the bodies of the obese are regarded as carcasses just as much as the bodies of anorexics and bulimics—obese bodies, however, are more of a "raw material" to be exploited than are the otherwise unprofitable and therefore disposable carcasses of anorexics and bulimics.

If the discourse of "carcass" seems offensive or too strong, keep in mind that its origin is the above referenced pharmaceutical study. Moreover, the ideas represented in such language are put into practice by corporations and research institutions when deadly conditions are not researched—and consequently people are allowed to die—because of a lack of potential profit. If the desire for money is a plausible account of some of the reasons for the minimal research into disordered eating, then the desire for money is an equally plausible explanation for the continuation of other practices that have questionable benefits and recognized risks; such is the case with gastric bypass surgery.

Evidence of the financial considerations at work in the proliferating of gastric bypass surgery is plainly offered in a recent article published in the *Journal of the American Medical Association*. Although it is an easy observation to miss, the authors take special care to note that the twofold increase in hospitalizations for people who undergo this procedure results in an even greater increase in health care costs. Careful examination reveals that the impact of these increased costs is, to say the least, financially alluring. For example, the average amount of money spent on hospitalizations by recipients of gastric bypass surgery during the three year period preceding surgery was $4,970; the average amount of money spent on hospitalizations by these same patients in the three year period following surgery was $20,651; and the average cost of the surgery itself is $33,672.[20] Thus, the average recipient of gastric bypass surgery is paying about $1,650 per year in hospital expenses before they undergo this procedure, and ends up paying about $6,900 per year in hospital expenses afterward—an increase of about $5,200 per year for at least three years. Keeping in mind that the estimated number of these procedures performed in 2005 is about 130,000 and that the average person pays more than $33,000 for the privilege of this "treatment," we can see precisely just how much the surgeons and facilities performing these procedures have gained in the last year alone. If each of these 130,000 gastric bypass patients paid the average cost for the procedure ($33,672) and experienced the average increase in medical expenses for the current year alone ($5,200), then the overall net gain for 2005 is an astounding $5 billion.[21]

It is little wonder that another recent study goes out of its way to mention with great specificity that "current estimates indicate that as little as 0.6% of patients who qualify for bariatric surgery undergo a bariatric surgical procedure in any given year."[22] What this means is that even though the performing of bariatric procedures currently constitutes a $5 billion per year industry, it has tapped less than one percent of its potential gains. We noted in the previous chapter that approximately 85 percent of all bariatric procedures are gastric bypass surgeries.[23] How much money is waiting to be made by performing gastric bypass surgeries? If everyone who is "qualified" for this procedure were to pay the requisite fees and subsequent rehospitalization costs, the money generated for a period of one year would total an amazing $710 billion![24] It would be difficult indeed to dismiss the financial motive for perpetuating an acknowledged risky procedure the efficacy of which has not been demonstrated in light of the extreme potential gains that it represents. The carcasses of the obese are a virtual gold mine.

The skeptical minded may be inclined to point out that, while it is not the most desirable characterization, in a capitalist economy—everyone's body is a carcass. Scientists and pharmaceutical companies, like everyone else, have to make money. Capitalism requires that less profitable opportunities get marginalized and more favorable ones get exploited. Like it or not (so the skeptic might suggest), eating disordered people are not victims of discrimination merely because they are treated as carcasses—every sick body is treated this way at some point in the medical/economic nexus. This by itself does not constitute any discrimination against the eating disordered.

In this last claim, of course, the skeptic would be correct. It is not, however, the mere discourse of "carcass" which necessitates the term discrimination here. "Discrimination" is a label which results from the unavoidable fact that only other people's carcasses are researched, effectively treated, and healed. Eating disordered carcasses are unresearched, treatments have little or no demonstrated efficacy, and we are permitted to die when profits lag and exploited as raw material when profits look promising. While it is unclear how the skeptical minded might find comfort in observing that people are dehumanized indiscriminately, it is still clear that—after this fact—eating disordered persons are treated very differently indeed.

There is much in our concrete experience which confirms what we have already detailed at the level of research—that at all levels of involvement in the medical domain, people with disordered eating are treated in a way that fundamentally differs from how others are treated. Discrimination occurs nationally in the research labs, and it is a pervasive part of local life as well. Again, this fact will be an obvious one to the eating disordered reader, and a not so obvious one to the "normal eater." What follows, then, is some detailed discussion of how people with disordered eating are singled out and treated differently within the context of everyday healthcare experience.

One place where our "singled out" status is more readily observable to the normal eater would be the place(s) where we receive treatment, such as it is. In some cases, it is the form of the treatment which portends a unique attitude towards the eating disordered—such is the case with gastric bypass surgery. We've already noted the tremendous potential for monetary gain that this procedure represents. The basic principle on which this treatment is founded, however, also indicates questionable thinking. The rationale for gastric by-pass surgery goes something like this: in order to arrest the patient's propensity for overindulgence in food, a significant portion of the stomach is removed. But the only way that this could be construed as a possible remedy is if it is also believed that once the organ which processes a certain substance is reduced in its capacity, the person will cease to overindulge in that substance. It is obvious enough, however, that no one in the medical field believes this to be true. If it were actually believed that a reduced processing organ would reduce indulgence in the substance processed, then we would be treating alcoholism by removing portions of the alcoholic's liver before it became cirrhotic, and we would be treating smokers by removing portions of their lungs while their lungs were yet healthy, etc. What we see here is a truly anomalous form of treatment—it arises from irrational thinking that is not applied to other similar conditions, it has no demonstrated efficacy in alleviating the symptoms it is intended to address and often makes people sicker, and we do it anyway. People with disordered eating are singled out and treated differently.

Aside from the form of thinking and its resulting attempts at treatment, there are other actual practices which belie a different attitude towards eating disorders than other relevantly similar conditions. Casual visits to any large hospital, even a mere drive past their entrance(s), can be revealing in this regard. It is common to see people congregated outside the doorways of these facilities—smoking cigarettes. Some of the smokers are employees (nurses, staff, etc.), and some of the smokers are ambulatory patients. Patients—people being treated for all manner of illnesses, including various forms of cancer—are permitted to walk outside the hospital, smoke some cigarettes, and then return to their program of treatment. People often frown on this behavior, many people think that it is irrational and stupid to take a smoke-break from chemotherapy or radiation or some other cancer treatment, but this is in fact permitted at many hospitals. Some hospitals have begun to reform these permissive policies by restricting cigarette smoking on their "campuses," but many employees and patients circumvent these restrictions simply by walking across the street to smoke. It seems fairly obvious, then, that the restrictions are not intended to curtail smoking by patients, but rather are supposed to reduce the amount of allegedly deadly secondhand smoke that innocent bystanders are forced to inhale.

It is unimaginable, however, that these same freedoms so liberally granted to smokers should be extended to eating disordered persons even at a single treatment center. The very thought of a binge eater meandering across the street to the buffet or a bulimic crossing the street for a vomit-break is completely foreign to this environment and appears an altogether silly suggestion. Why is it that cancer patients are freely permitted to ingest a substance that we know has *caused* the very disease for which they are being treated, while at the same time people with disordered eating are forbidden to express even a *symptom* of their condition? Eating disordered people are singled out and treated differently.

Proceed now through the entrance to the treatment facility and see how the situation progresses. Eating disorders are widely held to be addictions, but those of us who are addicted to our disordered eating behaviors are not treated according to the principles by which other addicts are treated. Despite the often noted similarities between these conditions, the hospital experience of the anorexic is very different indeed from that of the addict. When, for example, alcoholics show up in an emergency room or a detoxification facility, they can legally be held (against their wills) only until such time as they are sober. Even though sobriety in no way indicates that the medical problems associated with alcoholism have abated, and even though sobriety is never taken as indicating a cessation to one's drinking (or even a desire to stop), short-term sobriety by itself is usually enough to get one released from an emergency room or detoxification facility or "drunk tank," provided that one has not committed any crimes.

Anorexics can also be legally held against their wills. But when anorexics find themselves similarly detained in a psychiatric facility, eating a good breakfast does not constitute a sufficient condition for release. To be released from facilities similar to those geared for detoxing alcoholics, anorexics must not only get "sober" with food (that is, eat), but must also demonstrate a "willingness" to continue eating and must be medically evaluated and found relatively free of complications associated with their condition. "Food-sobriety" alone will not get one released. If these two conditions are perceived by the medical community to be relevantly similar with respect to their addictive characteristics and associated health risks and high rates of recidivism, then why are the conditions and experiences of those who are treated so vastly dissimilar? Why do we not detain alcoholic patients, for example, until their liver enzymes are within normal parameters, and yet routinely detain bulimic patients until their electrolytes are properly balanced? People with disordered eating are singled out and treated differently.

The reasons which are used to justify court ordered institutionalization, extended detention, restraint, and involuntary "re-feeding" for persons with disordered eating are applicable in equal or greater measure to numerous other identifiable behaviors which are no less risky to one's health than the behaviors of the anorexic, bulimic, or binge eater. These other behaviors, however, are rarely met with the paternalism and condescending institutional restrictions and confinements in which we are often expected to recover. The wearing of motorcycle helmets, for example, has been a contentious issue in many states. A significant number of helmet laws that have been passed, however, have subsequently been repealed. The principal reason for these repeals? Riders don't like to wear helmets, and legislators are willing to allow riders to take the risk of riding without them.

Upon careful examination, one finds that all the arguments which seem to justify court ordered incarcerations and/or force-feedings of eating disordered persons have an even greater application to the issue of wearing motorcycle helmets. The injuries sustained from either of these risky behaviors can be serious and life threatening, society has an interest in minimizing these injuries as the cost of medical treatment must often be borne by publicly funded or non-profit hospitals, and the risk-taking behavior affects other people along with the risk-taker. In short, the reasons that are given in favor of court ordered medical and/or psychiatric treatment of the eating disordered are precisely the same as those which have been used as a foundation for helmet laws. These two behaviors—helmetless riding and disordered eating—are relevantly similar with respect to the ways that we reason about them.

Legislators in many states have demonstrated a great willingness to scuttle helmet laws solely on the bases of rider dislike and non-compliance. When motorcycle riders rebel against restrictions on their risk-taking, it is widely regarded as an expression of freedom. When we eating disordered are non-compliant with our tube-feedings, weigh-ins, and dietary demands, however, this is not taken to be an expression of freedom at all, but rather is seen as further justification for the restrictive and coercive treatments being imposed on us. Apparently, disordered eating does not get one confined simply because it involves great risks to one's health, or because it is costly to treat the medical conditions that often result, or because it affects those close to the disordered person. If these were the principal reasons for involuntary institutionalizing and forced treatment, then many other persons would fall under their purview; helmetless riders, cigarette smokers, sky-divers, the sexually promiscuous, etc. People with disordered eating are singled out and treated differently.

We accrue specific identifiable disadvantages by virtue of being eating disordered. These disadvantages extend well beyond what is directly attributable to the conditions and behaviors from which we suffer. Since these disadvantages reflect a status that is comparatively lower or de-graded relative to others in similar situations, these disadvantages are political. The fact that we are not tallied so as to get an accurate read on the prevalence of our condition is the result of a political decision, it is not a symptom of our unhealthy behavior. Similarly, the fact that there is no accepted model for treating disordered eating is not a result of any of the essential features of these disorders themselves, but is rather a result of the dominant attitudes surrounding us as a group. We bear striking resemblances to many other sufferers of many other conditions, and yet, at every level of the healthcare system, the treatment we receive fails to reflect those similarities. In addition to all of the potentially miserable features of the disorder itself, being eating disordered places one at a significant disadvantage relative to those who are not eating disordered.

When one accrues significant disadvantages solely by virtue of being part of a group, the group is said to be oppressed. When one's situation is similar to the situations of others, one merits being treated in ways similar to how others are treated. To lose this legitimate claim to similar treatment as a result of one's inclusion in a group provides the basis for asserting that the group in question is oppressed. This is the very meaning of claiming, for example, that non-whites are oppressed in the United States. It is by way of this understanding that women can reasonably be said to constitute an oppressed group. As an even clearer example, we find that gays and lesbians often accrue significant legal disadvantages (lack of marital privileges, equal opportunity in housing, employment, adoption of children, etc.), not because they break the law, but because they are gay or lesbian—and this constitutes oppression. *The whole point of this book is to bring to light that the discourse of oppression is applicable to the eating disordered, and that this discourse must be applied to us as a group if we are to recover from our disordered eating.*

The task of making a case for our oppressed status is both an easy one and a difficult one. The easy part is making the case to our eating disordered sisters and brothers. Most of us have a multitude of lived experiences which confirm that recovery is not the norm, and we have little trouble recognizing the relationship between recovery rates, research funding, treatment options, and basic respect for us as human beings. The hard part is making the case to people who are not eating disordered. History demonstrates that people whose life experiences are principally outside the constraints of oppression tend to have great difficulty in recognizing the painful reality of oppression. White people, for example, have great difficulty in being able to recognize and acknowledge the reality of white privilege. It is a laborious endeavor indeed for men to accept that women are often politically and economically disadvantaged. To the vast majority of heterosexuals, the belief that "it's fine to be gay, as long as people keep it to themselves" does not seem at all oppressive.

It is important to remember at this point that we are trying to focus on the eating disordered. The agenda in this chapter is not to persuade the reader that racial minorities, women, and gays are all oppressed—go ahead and reject all those claims if it seems better to do so. The point here is to see clearly what the mechanics of oppression look like, to understand what it means to call a group oppressed, and to note that people outside the oppressed group often have exceptional resistances to acknowledging that oppression exists. One can certainly understand the meaning and political dynamic of this label without having to debate its applicability in particular situations outside the parameters of our general discussion of eating disorders.

Suppose, for the sake of the argument, that we never convince any normal eaters of our oppressed status. It matters not whether our failure is attributable to our own lack of effort or our being deceived into thinking that we really aren't oppressed after all. What if we just don't make a case for ourselves in this regard? The inevitable result of our silence, whatever its motive, is that nothing changes; research funds are left at 1.5 percent, new research is not begun, no accepted model of treatment emerges and questionable treatments continue to proliferate, and we continue to die. *That's what silence reaps, more dead anorexic, bulimic, and binge-eating sisters and brothers.*

Sisters and brothers? Yes, the terms are used here in the context of political solidarity, but they mean more than that—these are familial terms. Who among us can honestly say "I'm the only eating disordered person in my family"? We may not yet understand the precise mechanism by which our conditions pervade blood relations (let's give the good folks at the University of Pittsburgh genome study a little time to sort it out), but our experience confirms that eating disorders—unlike lightning—seldom strike but once. If we fail to advocate for ourselves, demand that we be recognized, counted, researched, treated and healed, then we leave our disordered eating to our future generations. It is already plain enough that few normal eaters are going advocate on our behalf, the people best suited to do so (the NIH, NIMH, CDC, and USDA) have flatly refused. So, as difficult a demand as it is, *we have to come out.*

This is indeed a difficult demand, as there is great stigma attached to being eating disordered in our culture. The disgrace and shame that are attached to our "disease" reflect a collection of social attitudes which serve to keep us silent. There is relatively little or no stigma attached to having other life-threatening conditions. Ordinarily, when someone tells us that they have a severe illness, we feel sympathy and are often motivated to offer help in any way we can. This presence of healthy sympathy and lack of stigma serve to facilitate a person's being able to ask for help as well as the ability of others to give it. The fact that eating disorders engender a very different response indicates that the cultural framework in which we share this kind of personal information is twisted so as to facilitate sympathy and aid for some people— but not others.

To be sure, we eating disordered are denied adequate healthcare. We are denied the care necessary to heal us not because we can't pay for it, nor because we are criminals—we are denied the means by which to recover *because we are eating disordered.* Again, those who are skeptical will want to point out that in fact eating disordered persons have recovered. So why, it might be asked, would someone believe that healthcare is denied us? The answer is that

recovery is the anomaly rather than the norm. In the treatment of all other medical conditions, we desire the norm to be recovery. But it is different regarding
the treatment of disordered eating. Our healthcare system promulgates the notion that rare or occasional recovery is sufficient, and it does so by allocating
us minimal research funds, by refusing to acknowledge our numbers, and by
enforcing highly questionable practices of inefficient treatment, restraint, and
confinement against us that are not similarly enforced in connection with other
medical conditions. By analogy, simply noting that there were in fact a few
published female authors in 18th century Europe would not demonstrate that
women received opportunity and education equal to their male counterparts at
that time. More formally, noting the exception does not disprove the rule—
rather, it confirms it. Yes, some of us recover. But we do so against incredible
odds. While this is to be celebrated and investigated (and we will do so in the
next chapter), it does not provide evidence contrary to our oppression.

Noting that there are people enjoying prolonged recovery from disordered
eating provides another reason for why it is that we have to come out—we
need to enlighten the medical community as to the meaning of being eating
disordered and the means of recovery. The current situation is such that many
millions of people suffer from disordered eating, and we have no established
reliable means by which to arrest the progression of their disorder and alleviate their symptoms. But since there are a few cases in which people have gotten better anyway, we should try and learn what we can from their experiences. Empirical scientists often investigate in this manner; some events are
observed the causes of which want to be known. Since the outcome is similar in the events being observed, we attempt to discover something similar in
the surrounding and antecedent conditions of each event. If several people in
a small locale all end up with food poisoning, for example, we try to find out
the source of the illness by asking them what they ate and then discerning
some common feature among the data that we are given. Similarly, if several
people manage to put together some long-term recovery from disordered eating, we should ask them how they understood this to happen, and we would
ask this not for the purpose of writing a best selling "my experience with bulimia" book, but rather to discern some common features of recovery.

Thus far, the minimal research that has been conducted has focused solely
on attempts to discover causes (or "risk factors") for the disordered behaviors
themselves. Although we have acquired some understanding of the complex
set of antecedent conditions which precipitate disordered eating, this approach has been a failure in pragmatic terms—there is no accepted treatment
method, and most people don't recover. The shift in perspective that we are
advancing here, then, is critically important. Rather than continue to investigate the causes of the disorder (an investigation that is barely being conducted

anyway), we need to investigate the conditions of recovery. If we had enough first person descriptions of what eating disorders look like from the inside, and what the personal mechanisms of recovery are, we could conceivably discern a general form (or set of forms) that recovery tends to take, and then, of course, seek measures to facilitate these conditions in others who still suffer.

Unfortunately, even the most well written and received accounts of suffering and recovery are not looked to for useful information beyond the level of pure content. The content of an eating disorder narrative may be its most outstanding and obvious feature to the non-eating disordered reader; normal eaters are often shocked, surprised, and disgusted to learn about what we do that makes us eating disordered. That supermarket tabloids can make a significant profit by sensationalizing celebrity eating disorders is a fact that speaks for itself. But there is nothing to be gained for us merely by shocking our oppressors with perversely entertaining details about how we go about practicing our illnesses and portrayals of ourselves solely as "victims of a disease." We want to enlighten— not entertain. These narratives need to be appropriated in a different way so as to reveal what sorts of conditions in the lives of eating disordered people can reasonably be understood as facilitating long-term recovery.

For us, therefore, coming out involves more than just telling people that we are eating disordered. It involves telling healthcare providers where we are on the continuum of recovery (even if we are at the very beginning) and how we got there. The more information we give of this kind, the more we have to work with in understanding where recovery comes from. In this way, coming out provides new terrain and a new model for eating disorders research.

We have to come out. The shame and stigma of having an eating disorder are not products of the disorder itself but are superimposed over the condition by an uncaring and unsympathetic cultural framework. To realize this, that an eating disorder is not shameful or disgraceful, is to be freed from the stigma that surrounds us. To realize that our condition is not the symbol of a lesser being is to be able to speak of it out loud. Speaking out about eating disorders with no shame whatsoever makes it very plain to the listener that the stigma associated with us has its roots in the oppressive system in which we are forced to recover, but that having an eating disorder itself is no source of disgrace. It may be true that the dominant attitudes in our culture would place guilt or blame on some people solely because they suffer from a particular medical condition, but we do not have to accept this. We have the ability to reject it, and we do reject it every time we speak out loud about our eating disorders.

And when we speak out loud, all 27 million of us, we will be heard. We are not helpless victims after all, we have the ability to *exploit our prevalence* and overwhelm the system. 27 million people is a lot of people to accommodate. Think of what the scenario could become if every eating disordered person were to come out, self-identify and demand treatment. Healthcare in the United States would be in an immediate state of crisis and would, therefore, be forced to deal with the reality of our epidemic and untreated suffering. Coming out has the volatile potential to facilitate—*en masse*—the means of securing long-term recognition and recovery for us and for future generations.

Few people have blazed a trail for us at this point. There are, of course, people of celebrity status who are known to struggle (or to have struggled) with eating disorders, but they tend to speak of these things very little. The best known cases of eating disordered celebrities, unfortunately, are the ones who did not survive their illness. And in these cases, the trail was not so much blazed by someone who was outspoken about eating disorders as it was by someone who was a casualty of an irresponsible health care system. It is little wonder, then, that it may be more difficult today to come out about one's bulimia or anorexia or binge eating than it is to come out about being gay or lesbian—we don't have a Harry Hay—yet.[25] Our purposes would probably be best served if we all became a collective Harry Hay.

Granted, the coming out analogy has its limits. Harry Hay was coming out with a goal of getting the gay community to be treated as something other than ill, to get homosexuality out of the DSM. We are coming out for what may be thought of as the opposite reasons; we want the medical aspects of our disordered eating to be treated as such, we need our DSM-IV criteria to be taken more seriously. Aside from these differences of particular circumstance, however, we do have a similar agenda which is to be treated with an equal share of the respect and compassion which all people deserve. Would that we had someone who is as openly bulimic or anorexic as Harry Hay was openly gay—not to celebrate any of their suffering or ill-health, but certainly to boast a lack of shame about being eating disordered and some success in recovery. Can you imagine what it would mean to someone suffering in silence and isolation with the misery of an active eating disorder to become aware of a visible public person who was not only enjoying a long-term recovery but also outspokenly proud to be eating disordered? A few such people would go a long way in generating some awareness of our existence and oppression in the consciousness of a culture that has too long turned a blind eye to our silent suffering. *Manifesto!*

This business of coming out is a fearsome prospect indeed and more needs to be said about it in order to make a case for its feasibility and desirability for us. To be sure, our concern for future generations provides considerable motive to begin talking about our eating disorders in a loud-mouthed way. We need to be loud-mouthed so that our children and grandchildren might be spared some measure of the eating disordered misery from which we have been left unattended, to navigate and eventually die. Obviously of great concern to us also, however, is how others' attitudes towards us will change once they know that we are eating disordered. Perhaps it is not so much the people around us (to whom we might come out) that make us feel reluctant, but rather the cultural attitudes that provide a framework for all our interactions—with other people, and with food. Fast food counters and all-you-can-eat buffets are, after all, the altars of our culture with respect to food; Guiness World Records reports that "In 2000, Americans spent over $110 billion on fast food, more than on higher education, personal computers, or new cars."[26] To starve or overeat or deliberately vomit is grossly to misuse the substance upon that altar and so allegedly proves that one is either immoral or unholy or perhaps completely stupid. Overindulgence is the norm, so much so that we no longer recognize the biological consequences of a life of overeating as symptoms of an illness at all—remember, obesity is not part of the DSM-IV diagnostic criteria for disordered eating. To live in a culture where fast food and overindulgence are the dominant modes of consumption and come out as a bulimic or anorexic is an intimidating prospect.

It is the experience of many of us, however, that the majority of people to whom we come out, although surprised initially by the revelation, don't seem all that freaked out about it 24 hours later. More often than not, the fact that one is eating disordered goes unacknowledged forever after. This suggests three important things. First, the fear of being scrutinized or "on stage" that one has prior to telling someone about an eating disorder is usually worse than what actually happens, rather like waiting to receive an injection at the doctor's office.

Second, eating disorders feel like foreign territory to many people. They simply don't know what to say about the subject or how to feel about it. While silence may preserve the greatest degree of comfort for most normal eaters, this does seem a reliable indicator of the necessity of more discourse about eating disorders. If 90 percent of the population remains ignorant of the potentially terminal condition that afflicts the other 10 percent, the chances of survival of that 10 percent will not be able to improve.

Third, statistically, the chances of coming out to someone who's already similarly afflicted are about one in ten. Often, the people to whom we come out react with silence because they are not ready themselves to come out, and discussing it simply brings them too close to the issue.

The most common response to coming out to casual acquaintances, and often with people to whom one is close, is a brief acknowledgement at most. Sometimes it does in fact happen that people have strong negative responses to our eating disorders; "how could you do this to me?" or "how could you have kept this from me?" It is tempting in such cases to respond to such inquiries with retorts such as "I'm not purging your stomach, I'm purging mine" or "how could you not have noticed that I was so sick?" This kind of interaction, however, accomplishes little. The angry response to our coming out is still an indicator that the person doesn't want to talk about it or deal with it. They are simply being more direct in saying so than the person who responds minimally or with silence.

It is prudent, in light of these observations, to exercise some forethought and practical judgment when deciding to whom one will come out. If the prospective recipient of your revelation has a propensity to respond to such things in a non-constructive manner, then come out to someone else first. Practice is very helpful in learning how to navigate the ways in which people respond to such disclosures, and it is helpful in learning how to navigate our own fears and misgivings about discussing our eating disorders openly and with pride rather than shame.

The internet is an ideal venue for discussing one's disordered eating anony-mously. There are a variety of facilities online which are used to discuss dis-ordered eating and other related topics. Many of these web-sites are routinely shut down (by well-meaning but overly fearful normal eaters), but new ones are always cropping up to take their place. Chapter five in this book devotes significant discussion to the controversy surrounding web-sites alleged to be "pro-anorexia" or "pro-bulimia." For the most part, however, media hype and warnings from professionals have been overstated and hyperbolic and are largely unwarranted and unwise. Pro-ED web-sites are no more risky than any other online discussion facility, and can be very helpful in this regard.

Sometimes our fears about coming out go beyond how people will respond to us or think of us afterwards. We are afraid of having to deal with our own disordered eating—or worse—having to enter the medical domain for treat-ment, perhaps even involuntarily. It may seem paradoxical that after seeing how obviously ineffective most treatment options are, and even how danger-ous a few of them are, that we should suggest taking action that could con-ceivably place one at the mercy of this same healthcare system. With care and forethought, however, this situation can be navigated successfully.

The first thing that one should note in this regard is that being open about one's eating disorder probably should have the *eventual* result of involving one in some kind of program of recovery. It would, after all, be quite unreasonable to expect those close to us to tolerate the disclosure of a life-threatening condi-tion while at the same time refusing all future programs of recovery. The point of coming out is to facilitate healing, and the first and most important step in our healing is exchanging the culturally imposed attitude of shame for one of pride. The second step in our healing is the shift from being eating disordered with terminal behavior to being eating disordered with healthy behavior.

We will, in chapter 5, pursue a detailed discussion of the meaning of pride in connection with eating disorders. At this point, however, we are simply noting that when we come out we need to be prepared to accept at least some amount of healing—even if that healing is not to be immediately reflected in our behavior. To refuse the very possibility of good health while at the same time disclosing behaviors that will inevitably result in one's ill health is probably unfair to the person with whom we're sharing. It places them in the awkward position of complicity with our worsening health and eventual death. One may, therefore, want to do some work on facilitating this shift—from embracing eating disordered sickness to accepting eating disordered health—in advance of coming out to those who are close or intimate. Perhaps you are engaged in such a project by virtue of reading this book . . . Remember, recovery is not so much a function of becoming non-eating-disordered as it is a function of how one's eating disordered self is manifest in the world. Coming out, therefore, is about connecting with those around us, it is not about admitting fault or wrong-doing.

"But what if they insist that I be institutionalized, etc.?" It takes significantly more than the insistence of a friend or family member to have someone involuntarily committed to an inpatient treatment program. Most states have strict criteria that must be met in order to obtain a court order for treatment, including signatures of multiple attending physicians and/or psychiatric experts as well as the consent of the treatment facility. Such signatures are usually obtainable only under conditions demonstrated to be "extreme" or "life-threatening." To be sure, many of us pass though some period of time where we meet these criteria, but we tend not to dwell in such a state permanently. This fear, therefore, although very real and quite severe in many people, is usually exaggerated. Nonetheless, this situation can easily be avoided in all but the most gravely extreme cases (in which others are likely to know what's going on anyway—whether you've come out or not) by seeking some help on one's own prior to coming out. In fact, being able to come out to another person and include in that sharing that one is already on the road to good health tends greatly to increase others' receptivity to what we say. This preemptive strategy affords one a great freedom in making treatment choices, from casual outpatient therapy to a more rigorous routine, from 12-step support and recovery groups to the advice of a physician. It also gives one some practice by coming out to people to whom one is less close. Freedom in making treatment choices, of course, doesn't guarantee that the chosen treatments will be effective. The point here, however, is not so much to be able to tell others that we are engaged in a *successful* program of recovery—the point is to be able to conjoin with one's coming out that one is actively seeking support of some kind. This will preclude the ability of others to seek involuntary institutionalization in nearly all cases, even when one's recovery is minimal or non-existent. Few if any treatment facilities will accept patients involuntarily when they are already known to be seeking treatment voluntarily.

If you are not ready to pursue any kind of recovery from disordered eating, then come out to others who are of a similar mind. This scenario is where on-line ED communities are particularly helpful; you can remain anonymous, maintain your current behaviors, and still connect with people in some respect. Connecting with people is the feature of coming out that turns out to be most helpful to us, whether we're changing our behavior or not. As a general guide, then, the "other" to whom one may come out can be discerned according to one's willingness to move in the direction of healthy eating.

What should be clear at this point is that this manifesto is not advocating a random or ill-prepared public discourse about one's eating disorder. The kind of coming out that is helpful is the kind that has some forethought about how it will be received, to whom it will be appropriate, and in what way it should be conjoined with other helpful information about one's own recovery as well as information about some helpful resources for friends and family. One cannot iron out all the possible wrinkles of a potential coming out, but one can avoid a lot of unnecessary difficulties if one prepares for it ahead of time in the ways mentioned here and in the next two chapters. And don't just rely on this manifesto, ask someone else who has already become comfortable with discussing their eating disorder for some advice and insight.

If one is mindful of these concerns, coming out accomplishes far more than we initially were after. Of course, we want to advocate for the eating disordered, overwhelm the system with our numbers, get counted after all and demand new options for reliable treatment, etc. And coming out will have the inevitable result of facilitating these things. Beyond these goals, however, we gain something personally from the experience. By preparing to come out, we begin a recovery—and beginning a recovery, no matter how modest or prolonged the beginning, is a monumental achievement. Moreover, we begin to connect with each other. The importance of this connecting cannot be overstated. The cultural attitudes that we've been discussing, evidenced in the profound silence of the medical community concerning our condition, creates in us the powerful and convincing illusion that we are alone in our suffering. Coming out dispels this imposed isolation and is itself a healing experience for us, no matter how it is received by others. It is precisely these healing qualities of coming out that constitute the topic for discussion in the next chapter.

NOTES

1. Centers for Disease Control and Prevention, "Efforts to Reduce or Prevent Obesity," available online: <http://www.cdc.gov/od/oc/media/pressrel/fs050419.htm> The article cited is K.M. Flegal, B.I. Graubard, D.F. Williamson, and M.H. Gail, "Excess Deaths Associated with Underweight, Overweight and Obesity," *Journal of the American Medical Association* 293 (2005): 1861–7.

2. Goliath Casket Company: <http://www.oversizecasket.com> See especially the article posted on the Goliath web-site entitled "U.S. Company Builds Seven-Foot Wide Coffin," <http://www.oversizecasket.com/articles/particle2.html>

3. Centers For Disease Control and Prevention, "Overweight and Obesity: Contributing Factors," 2005. <http://www.cdc.gov/nccdphp/dnpa/obesity/contributing _factors.htm>

4. See <http://mypyramid.gov>

5. See <http://mypyramid.gov/guidelines/index.html>

6. "Executive Summary of the Dietary Guidelines for Americans 2005," <http://www.health.gov/dietaryguidelines/dga2005/document/html/ executivesummary.htm>

7. "Executive Summary of the Dietary Guidelines."

8. "Dietary Guidelines for Americans, 2005," <http://www.health.gov/ dietaryguidelines/dga2005/document/pdf/DGA2005.pdf>

9. USDA "Press Release," April 19, 2005, <http://mypyramid.gov/global_nav/ media_press_release.html>

10. In fact the mortality rate for people with schizophrenia is somewhat higher than in the general population. This increased mortality is not, however, thought to be due to schizophrenia itself but rather to the increased rate of suicide among people with schizophrenia. For more information, see "Facts on Schizophrenia," published online by the Treatment Advocacy Center which is "a national nonprofit organization working to eliminate barriers to timely treatment of severe mental illness." <http:// www.psychlaws.org/GeneralResources/Fact5.htm>

11. Again, as with schizophrenia, bipolar disorder is associated with elevated mortality rates, but this is due to an increased risk of suicide rather than any essential feature of the disorder itself. According to the American Psychiatric Association: "Individuals with bipolar disorder repeatedly have been shown to have greater overall mortality than the general population. Although much of this risk reflects the higher rate of suicide." American Psychiatric Association, "Practice Guide for the Treatment of Patients with Bipolar Disorder (revision)," 2004. Available online: <http://www .psych.org/psych_pract/treatg/pg/bipolar_revisebook_3.cfm>

12. Admittedly, "autism" is a broad term which refers to a variety of conditions ranging quite widely with respect to severity. The point here is certainly not to suggest that autism is undeserving of research funds, but rather to note that there is no mortality rate which expresses the relative severity of all these conditions. The NIMH devotes a generous portion of its budget to "autism spectrum disorders," while at the same time presenting an awareness that even though some of these disorders present serious health risks no specific mortality rate has been demonstrated. At the same time, funds for eating disorders are almost non-existent, while the NIMH openly acknowledges the overwhelming mortality rates associated with them. For more information on autism spectrum disorders, see National Institute of Mental Health, "Autism Spectrum Disorders (Pervasive Developmental Disorders)," NIH Publication No.04-5511, 2004. <http://www.nimh.nih.gov/healthinformation/autismmenu.cfm>

13. S. Bogdanovic, *Opportunities In Obesity, Anorexia, and Bulimia: A Report for Scrip World Pharmaceutical News* (London: PJB Publications Ltd, 1992). List price: £300.

14. David Willman, "NIH Seeks 'Higher Standard,'" *Los Angeles Times*, 2 February 2005.

15. National Institutes of Health, "Summary of NIH-Specific Provisions in Interim Final Rule, Prohibited Outside Activities." Available online: <http://www.nih.gov/about/ethics/020105COIsummary.pdf>

16. "New rules at NIH anger its employees," *Washington Post*, 4 February 2005.

17. Irving Kent Loh, M.D., "Letter to the Editor: Ethics and Unintended Consequences," *Los Angeles Times*, 5 February 2005.

18. J.A. Guisado, F.J. Vaz, J.J. Lopez-Ibor, M.I. Lopez-Ibor, J. del Rio, and M.A. Rubio, "Gastric Surgery and Restraint from Food as Triggering Factors of Eating Disorders in Morbid Obesity," *International Journal of Eating Disorders* 31 (2002): 97–100.

19. D.S. Zingmond, M.L. McGory, and C.Y. Ko, "Hospitalization Before and After Gastric Bypass Surgery," *Journal of the American Medical Association* 294, no. 15 (2005): 1918–24.

20. "[M]ean hospital charges were $33672 for RYGB, $4970 for hospitalizations in the 3 years before RYGB, and $20651 for hospitalizations in the 3 years after RYGB." Zingmond, McGory, and Ko, "Hospitalization Before and After Gastric Bypass Surgery."

21. ($33,672 + $5,200) × 130,000 patients = $5,053,360,000

22. B.M. Wolfe and J.M. Morton, "Weighing in on Bariatric Surgery," *Journal of the American Medical Association* 294, no. 15 (2005): 1960–3.

23. H.P. Santry, D.L. Gillen, and D.S. Lauderdale, "Trends in Bariatric Surgical Procedures," *Journal of the American Medical Association* 294, no. 15 (2005); 1909–17.

24. If 130,000 procedures represents 0.6% of qualified individuals, then 1% of qualified individuals would be about 215,000. According to the information currently available in the above citations, there are therefore about 21.5 million individuals who are "qualified" for some form of bariatric procedure. Again, the research cited above asserts that about 85% of all bariatric procedures are gastric bypass surgeries. 85% of the 21.5 million qualified people amounts to 18,275,000 patients. Hence, it follows that ($33,672 + $5,200) × 18,275,000 million patients = $710,385,800,000.

25. Harry Hay (1912–2002) is usually acknowledged to have been the initiator of the gay liberation movement.

26. *Guiness World Records 2004* (London: Guiness World Records Limited, 2003).

Chapter Four

Radical Recovery: What It Means to Be Eating Disordered

It should be obvious that we need to understand what it means to be eating disordered. If we don't understand what it means to be eating disordered, then we won't be prepared to identify and treat people who suffer from disordered eating. We clearly aren't getting a useful model for gaining such understanding from current research and treatment practices, so we are going to have to provide a new model for understanding the meaning of being eating disordered *ourselves*. That's right, knowledge of eating disorders will have to come from the inside out, from those of us who are eating disordered. In providing this knowledge to caregivers, we will facilitate their ability effectively to treat us. At the same time, coming out is essential to our recovery on a personal level; coming out itself is therapeutic. One of the principal dilemmas of being eating disordered is that the dynamics of the disorder work in tandem with cultural stigmas to stifle the very coming out that we need in order to recover. It is with these thoughts in mind that this chapter attempts to speak clearly about eating disorders to anyone who has an interest in facilitating the healing of those who still suffer.

There is no good reason for thinking that people in the medical community suffer from disordered eating any more or any less than the rest of us. The medical community, therefore, appears to be in a position quite different from that of other communities with regard to these conditions—disordered eating is no more or less prevalent in the medical community than in other populations, but the medical community is exceptionally more burdened with the task of dealing with eating disordered people. Since this extra responsibility is not coincidental with any extra experience or "inside perspective," the burden of treating eating disordered patients must be borne by an expanded "external" understanding of these conditions.

Such is the case with nearly any identifiable malady, disease, or debilitating condition; doctors, nurses, therapists, and other medical personnel rarely draw on their own personal experience of suffering in establishing a treatment— they draw on the knowledge that they have acquired outside of (or external to) actually having the condition in question. Such knowledge is, for the most part, a product of scientific experimentation and medical research, and this is largely a good thing. If, for example, we only allowed people who actually had strokes to treat stroke patients, then there would be precious few people treating stroke patients. The fact that we can learn how to treat people with strokes without having to experience a stroke is to the significant advantage of the one who suffers a stroke.

But is it similarly advantageous to eating disordered patients to have people treating us who have collected their knowledge and expertise in this "external" manner? What are our chances of becoming healthy through medical treatments that are the result of an understanding which is predominantly external to the suffering it seeks to treat? Would our chances for such a recovery be improved if readily available treatment options were based on a different perspective—one which was significantly informed by an inside experiential understanding of eating disorders?

Only an examination of the current medical orthodoxy concerning eating disorders research, treatment options and treatment efficacy could answer such questions. And we have, in fact, conducted such an examination. Our investigation has demonstrated that there seems to be no motive whatsoever that would be sufficient to induce the medical research community to acquire adequate knowledge of eating disorders in the conventional experimental research-oriented method. Disordered eating constitutes the tenth leading cause of death in the United States, and yet our conditions are not being researched beyond the level of a token bare minimum. Our analysis has brought elements of our situation to the fore that should make people gasp in utter horror and grief: disordered eating affects more people in the United States than any other medical condition, disordered eating is more deadly than any other "mental illness" and the third most common chronic condition for adolescent females in the United States, and yet these conditions are virtually unresearched and have no accepted model for treatment.

It is therefore no great surprise that the "external" medical understanding of disordered eating is incoherent. Our eating patterns, for example, are thought to be excessively fragile such that one ought not let us even sniff a between meal snack, have lengthy conversations about diet programs, read fashion magazines, read or post to internet chat boards that may endorse our behavior, or ever use the bathroom after a meal without supervision. The temptation inherent in such situations is evidently perceived as threatening, as though we should be quarantined from these scenarios the way a person with a compromised immune system would be quarantined from germs.

Simultaneously, however, our eating habits are also characterized as being so deeply etched into us that we must occasionally be physically restrained and force-fed in order effectively to be treated. Eating disorders are often associated with either a most stubborn refusal to eat, or a refusal to stop eating, or a refusal to keep food in one's body long enough for it to be digested. Without such drastic measures, it is often contended, the eating disordered patient will surely revert back to their destructive tendencies.

Obviously, our eating is disordered when we suffer from these behaviors. But it should also be obvious that our eating cannot be brought into a state of "order" rather than "disorder" by treating it in such a contradictory manner. How is a patient's condition to be improved by treatment strategies that are rooted in this inconsistent frame of understanding? It is difficult indeed to imagine as successful the treating of disordered eating as though it is a delicately fragile routine that requires significant force and coercion in order to be changed.

When we cure cancer, we find out how the cancer works—its internal mechanisms, etc. In the absence of this internal understanding, we are lost. Fortunately, we can get this understanding from well funded and carefully thought out research. But we do not, for reasons already examined, obtain information about eating disorders in this way. We must therefore turn to the sufferers to provide the necessary internal perspective and transcend the purely speculative scientific model concerning these conditions.

Disordered eating affects the body but does not originate there. Whence comes this suggestion? It comes in the simple observation that although the body may be temporarily coerced into a healthy eating pattern, the unhealthy behaviors often return. Exceptionally high rates of recidivism and relapse confirm this painful fact. Conversely, it is also the case that the recovering person may be repeatedly physically tempted to relapse, yet without incident. The state or mode of an eating disorder, whether one is living in a healthy or unhealthy way, is only temporarily altered by coercive physical means.

Moreover, since the vast majority of patients relapse during their first year of recovery, it is legitimate to speak of coercive physical medical treatments as a form of *imposed dependence*. *Imposed* suggests that our treatments are often not of our own choosing. They are either involuntary or they are random guesses as to what will be effective. Neither coercion nor guesswork constitutes an informed or meaningfully free choice. *Dependence* suggests that the treatment we receive tends to create a future need for more treatment. We know that this is so because the recovery generated by available treatments is temporary, and in some scenarios the treatments make us sicker.

We who suffer from disordered eating are confused about food and termi-
nally dependent on our compulsions surrounding it. The system in which we
are supposed to find healing has consistently shown an effort to remedy our
situation by (a) further confusing us about food by instilling in us the notion
that our eating habits are fragile yet require great force to be changed, and (b)
imposing on us a situation of dependence by way of treatments that have only
short-term efficacy. It should be obvious that one is unlikely to recover from
any disorder by virtue of an equally disordered health care system.

Radical recovery is about learning to communicate. People who suffer
from disordered eating are fractured, divided or split into an internal domain
and an external domain. Eating disordered thinking often serves to set up (or
reinforce) what we hope will be impermeable boundaries—*walls*—that are
perceived to exist between one's inner private embodied conscious existence,
and everything else which lies outside (outward appearances, other people,
the external environment, etc.). Communication, in any form, involves a dialogue between these inner and outer domains, a connection between internal
states of consciousness and the external world that surrounds us. But in cases
of severe suffering from disordered eating, such communication has been cut
off or significantly impaired. Recovery, then, is about facilitating a reconnection and reintegration of what the sufferer experiences as fractured, separate
and distinct; the internal life of the self and the rest of the world that is external to that privately accessed self.

Many situations can become catalysts for this boundary which marks off
the self. For the most part, we are responding to what we experience as threatening, inappropriate, encroaching, or fearsome. Physical or psychological
abuses, for example, are certainly encroachments on an otherwise healthy understanding of self. Perhaps we were never abused in the strict sense of the
word, but we were harshly criticized or ridiculed because we were perceived
as unmotivated, sensitive, introverted, or "serious." Many of us have felt culturally out of place, finding the pressure to conform to certain ideals (with
which we intuitively disagreed) to be severe and unrelenting. We may in fact
have been endowed with all manner of natural gifts such as athleticism, in-
tellect, or musical talent, but found the cultural use of such gifts as a measure
of a person's worth to be inappropriate. We may have been naturally constituted with a sympathy for those who are less fortunate than ourselves, and
found our society's obsession with over-consumption and affluence to be fundamentally unbalanced and improper. We may have found life in a secular society to lack a spiritual element we felt we needed, or we may have felt that
life in a religious environment was overly harsh and rigid. We may not
presently be able to identify a specific element of our external environment
that is experienced as encroaching, we just feel encroached upon. Whatever

our individual circumstances, we have marked off the outside world in an effort to reestablish certain boundaries that were—in our experience—ignored, overstepped, or in some way imposed upon, pressured or violated, to defend a self that was experiencing some kind of threat or pain from an external source. We have reacted to the perceived severity of these experiences, however, by setting up equally severe boundaries around our selves, and we have become trapped by our own defense mechanisms.

We are sensitive to what we might refer to as pathological elements of our culture, environment, world, or family—and we, therefore, engage in a pathological detachment from these external domains. It is often a healthy and valuable asset to society that people refuse to accept its tenets or norms without critical evaluation, and so there is—somewhere in the eating disordered experience—the grounds for a sense of pride over not having consented to what we find wrong or offensive or inappropriate, even when we can't specifically articulate what it is. ED pride is the subject of the next chapter, but it is relevant at least to mention it here since the origins of disordered eating are, for a great many of us, significantly rooted in an otherwise virtuous refusal to accept what we feel or believe to be disordered social norms. Again, our problem is not our critical attitude toward the world that surrounds us (normal eaters often refer to this with the pejorative term "perfectionism"), our problem is that we translate this attitude into behavior that harms us rather than focusing it in a positive direction.

It should also be noted that what is experienced by the person who copes in this way may not seem harsh, or threatening, or abusive, etc., to an observer who is external or "objective." The point is that in each case the person in question—the subject—experiences things in this way. We cope with and/or defend ourselves against what we experience as an external threat to our internal sense of self and what is right. This method of coping clearly draws its strength not so much from its infallible accuracy as from setting up what are believed and hoped to be boundaries that are less permeable than the ones which formerly permitted the painful experiences we're trying to avoid.

People often mistake disordered eating as an attempt at self harm. Disordered eating is harmful, but it is not an attempt at self harm. Disordered eating reflects an attempt to avoid, control, or keep at safe distance what we believe will be harmful, painful, uncomfortable, or morally disagreeable. As the experience of pain often results in protective behavior, we monitor closely the distance that we create as a buffer between the "internal" and the "external," making sure that only safe, agreeable, painless material can traverse this neutral area and "get in." This is our mode of self defense, not self harm; the entire self as it were is covered with a protective scab so that what was once in pain will not be prodded into any new discomfort.

One may well ask how is it that something which is obviously harmful to one's self could possibly be thought of as a mechanism of self defense. Every one of us who has entered the healthcare arena for any kind of treatment has been asked this question at one time or another by a caring and yet otherwise clueless healthcare provider—"don't you understand that what you're doing is harmful and might kill you?" Yes, we understand that this is so. At the same time, however, our disordered eating is a defense mechanism that we believe will spare us more pain than it will cause. Physicians, nurses, and therapists often appear mystified by this belief, as though it is completely foreign to the medical frame of mind to defend against one kind of harm by potentially causing another. These same people, however, appear to have no misgivings about inflicting a prolonged chemotherapy on a cancer patient—a process that is specifically designed to prevent one kind of harm by causing another that is thought to be less severe. Moreover, many physicians actually endorse treatments that are known to cause *more* harm than they prevent; such has already been demonstrated with regard to the effects of gastric bypass surgery and involuntary institutionalization as it affects anorexics.

So, why is it that our healthcare providers cannot see their own most basic logic reflected in our disordered eating? The principal reason for this lack of understanding is twofold: we rarely attempt to articulate the protective benefits we accrue from our disordered eating, and our healthcare providers rarely listen to us when we do speak of such things. Our silence and the lack of listening on the part of those who provide our "treatment" serve to reinforce each other. The less we say, the less it is even possible for others to listen to us; and conversely, the less we are taken seriously when we speak, the less likely we are to try and articulate what we are experiencing. The history of the treatment of disordered eating is such that healthcare providers have had no real obligation to listen to our own descriptions of eating disordered experience, and such consideration may even be thought of as proscribed if for no other reason than that we are officially classified as "mentally ill." Doctors do not seek advice on the treatment of a particular insanity by first consulting someone who is afflicted with it . . .

Our acquiescing to this model and keeping silent, as noted in the previous chapter, has played a major role in the perpetuation of disordered eating. Although it may make sense conceptually to disregard the insights of the "mentally ill" regarding their own conditions, this strategy has been a failure for those of us with disordered eating. Healthcare providers have nothing to lose by giving serious consideration to what we have to say about our disordered eating, and we have nothing to lose by demanding that they listen to us. We already have the highest mortality for any condition listed in the DSM-IV. One would think that admitting failure and listening to our descriptions of disordered eating and recovery would be a simple matter for those currently responsible for our treatment. If it is not simple, then we have to demand it; *we talk, you listen!*

Food naturally becomes a focal point when one's internal private domain has been so marked off and distinguished from "external" sources of experience. Our survival depends upon the intake of food—food must cross the divide from the "external" to the "internal" on a daily basis. But the coping mechanism which has been so meticulously erected cannot let things pass into the self freely and unchecked. Food must pass into the self in as intimate a way as possible—it must enter the body. And so food intake must be very closely monitored and controlled indeed.

In the case of overeating, food is a focal point in a different way. Food intake serves to reinforce the protective boundaries between self and other by functioning as a surrogate other so that real others need not be encountered as much or as intimately. Excess food also leads to the eventual consequence of an actual physical barrier which helps insulate the self against unwanted intrusions from the outside—excess weight.

In these extreme modes of disordered eating, then, food is seen as an immigrant to be regarded with suspicion, and it is seen as providing insulation from an external world that is to be regarded with suspicion. Food becomes the focal point for the borderland between the internal and the external. Food constitutes the self's moat. It is perceived as a potential danger because it is an unavoidable emissary from an external and sometimes painful domain, and it is also the barrier which keeps at bay all such unwanted emissaries. In this way, the body in turn becomes increasingly identified with the self; one comes to think of oneself as a *body-self.*

Suspicion and avoidance of the world outside the body-self have shown themselves to manifest in a restrictive mode and an indulgent mode. When such restriction and indulgence find their principal focus and exercise in connection with one's eating habits, then one's eating becomes disordered—this is the meaning of the condition.

In its restrictive mode, this suspicion tries to exert control over (or even keep out) as much as it can from the world outside the body-self. Not only is that external domain the source of some experience perceived as painful or in some way disagreeable, but the physical matter (food) which must periodically enter therefrom has a transformative effect on the body-self (weight gain). And this natural consequence of eating is feared as having the added result of making the external world even more unfriendly. There are numerous reinforcements for this belief in our culture, notably those media presentations of what constitutes an acceptable or desirable body. Not only does the close monitoring of food intake provide some perceived security from an allegedly unfriendly domain, but it has the added benefit of making one's body-self more favorably regarded. In restriction, I guard myself from external forces and I endear myself to their aesthetic expectations simultaneously. In anorexia, I refuse altogether the advances of external matter into my body-self, I exert my self-control and become impenetrable. In bulimia, I routinely give in to the inviting quality of the matter that seeks to enter the body-self, but I will not allow it to stay. I dare the food to come in and gain me weight, but I get the last word by expelling it. I am penetrable, but only temporarily and only according to my own desires.

In binge eating I seek to accomplish the same goal—impenetrability—albeit by way of a different means. The goal, of course, is protection from an external domain that is experienced as threatening. Rather than gaining this surrogate feeling of protection by keeping food out, however, the transformative effect of weight gain that food has on the body-self is exploited for the sake of its consequence—keeping others at a distance.

In either mode, restriction or indulgence (anorexia, bulimia, or binge eating), the same effect can be achieved. Although the means appear contradictory, their common goal of protection provides for the possibility of one body-self suffering multiple and varying manifestations of disordered eating.

In a culture in which women are regarded as commodities by male consumers—principally in the multi-billion dollar industries of fashion, media advertising, and pornography—the metaphor of making oneself impenetrable carries especially significant importance. We should expect, based on the phenomenology of inner experience being offered here, that women are more susceptible to disordered eating than men are, if for no other reason than that women are encroached upon to a far greater degree than are men in our culture. Moreover, insofar as the physical abuse of children and their being deliberately targeted by all manner of media advertising is a readily observable problem in our culture, we should expect that younger people would be especially susceptible to disordered eating. Elderly people, as noted in the first chapter, are a nearly invisible sub-category of eating disordered persons. We know also that obesity is strongly correlated with poverty. Disordered eating, therefore, appears to manifest itself amidst an observable disempowering of people. Again, that our healthcare system should continually observe that women are afflicted disproportionately with disordered eating, and that the average age of onset is between 14 and 18, and that the poor are more likely to be obese, and yet claim that the reasons for these facts are not understood only serves as further evidence that what we have to say about our experiences is not taken seriously.

It is testimony to the fear and pain that we associate with the world external to our body-selves that we disconnect from that world by way of these miserable practices. There is some debate as to whether or not people choose to be eating disordered. It is not obvious, however, why an answer to this question would be important or even relevant in deciding whether or not to listen to what we have to say about our experiences. One never hears, for example, physicians requiring an answer to the question of whether or not people choose to smoke cigarettes prior to conducting research and deciding how to treat patients with lung cancer, or insisting that the "free will" of the alcoholic be philosophically assessed prior to deciding how best to treat cirrhosis of the liver. What seems at least initially obvious is that we do not choose to maintain this way of life in any usual sense of "choosing." One way of explaining this is to note that once our disordered eating becomes a routine for us, it quickly becomes an addiction—psychological as well as physical. The addictive character of these behaviors has been widely recognized and is relatively simple to explain.

Psychological addiction results from the simple fact that these behaviors are extremely effective in achieving their goal—a feeling of control with regard to how the outside world affects us. If I use food as a representation of all that must pass from the external world into my body-self, then strict control of my food intake will provide a strong feeling of mastery over that external domain. Conversely, if I live in a culture where obesity is closely associated with what is undesirable and ugly, then my obesity will be enough by itself to keep the external world at a comfortable distance.

Such feelings of mastery and/or comfort provide quick and significant reinforcement of the behavior in question. In combination with this, restrictive eating disorders often result in social reinforcement when a particularly thin body image is achieved as a result of starving or purging. I get what I need from it, so I do it again.

These artificially induced (yet truly experienced) emotions of confidence, acceptance, protection, comfort, control, and relief from anxiety are coupled with physiological responses that also serve to reinforce the focus on food as a coping mechanism. Many people with disordered eating speak of the experiences of a food high, a food hang-over, or similar feelings in connection with starving and purging. The physical sensations can be similar to an endorphin high, or a narcotic numbness. These chemical responses and their associated sensations are highly addictive.

Suffering from disordered eating, then, reflects a condensation of at least these two important aspects of experience onto a common surface; the experience of control over the boundary between body-self and other achieved by over-focusing on food, and the multitude of reinforcements (psychological, physical, and social) that often follow.

Within this dialectic of internal and external, we find that *place* is a valuable contributor in giving an account of the meaning and experience of eating disorders. Empirical explanations of events tend to draw heavily on time-based thinking or logic, searching for antecedent conditions in order to give an account of what is presently observed. The explanation we are proposing here, however, focuses not so much on the antecedent conditions of the disorder, but on its concrete physical embodied *spatial* manifestation. To be sure, disordered eating has antecedent conditions, and in many cases (or perhaps all cases) it will be helpful to have as much knowledge of these antecedent conditions as possible. This account does not deny the existence or usefulness of an awareness of prior conditions, but seeks rather to provide a most important missing ingredient—*place.*

There are conditions that can be described as prior to the disorder, and there are conditions that we can characterize as either internal or external to the sufferer. The discourse of the internal and the external cannot be reduced to an explanation which relies solely upon the discourse of antecedent conditions. Conversely, antecedent conditions cannot be fully accounted for solely within the dialectic framework of the internal and the external. An understanding of eating disorders which acknowledges only one of these modes of discourse, then, is significantly reduced in its efficacy and helpfulness—as we have seen and are now seeing in the medical world.

We do not suffer the torment of our disordered eating because of abstract causal principles. That is why we are hard pressed to answer doctors and family members when they ask us "why?" The suffering of these behaviors is not exclusively a function of how the present is related to some past condition, it is also (and perhaps especially) a function of my body-self and its relation to the rest of the world.

Again, this may provide some understanding as to why it is that women seem to suffer these illnesses more than men. Beginning with Carol Gilligan's ground-breaking work, a number of feminist thinkers in the last generation have given significant attention to the many ways in which female psychology and reasoning differ from that of males.[1] One area of considerable interest (notably articulated in Gilligan's work, and elsewhere in feminist psychology and philosophy) suggests that while men tend to think in ways characterized as linear and temporal, women tend to understand the world as a web of relations—drawing heavily on a logic that is embodied and spatial. These are, of course, generalizations rather than absolutes. There are lots of eating disordered men, and there are lots of women who eat in a healthy way. A significant trend, however, is that women suffer more from disordered eating than men do, and their predominantly male doctors can't understand the suffering well enough to provide much of any relief. In light of this observable trend that women suffer and men fail in their charge to provide medical care and relief, ignoring these gender differences would be irresponsible indeed.

Male physicians often try to convince women that eating disorders are "precipitated" by certain cultural factors which place undue pressure on women to conform to unrealistic body-images, and that it would be in their best interest if women learned not to take these unrealistic images of beauty so seriously. Cultural beliefs about ideal body-types are certainly at work in the perpetuating of disordered eating. When male doctors tell women not to take these cultural beliefs so seriously, however, they fail to take into account two important points. The first is that it is men who created most of these images in the first place. Presumably, if men didn't really want women to take seriously the pervasive images of desperately thin women as attractive, then men wouldn't create and surround themselves with these images. Secondly, the "don't take it so seriously" line fails to take into account the possibility that women, as women, may in fact take more seriously a physical embodied spatial form of thinking. Being male myself, I can't push this point too much, but will have to let others address it more directly. But until this happens, doctors (especially male doctors) will have to give female eating disordered patients the benefit of the doubt and not simply parrot the CDC "make better choices" advice in a conceptual package—"you need to think better thoughts." It is not so much our thinking that needs to be changed as it is our behavior.

The explanatory model being proposed here—the mal-adapting of the dialectic interchange between self and world—has the notable advantage of being able to account for more of the phenomena associated with eating disorders than does the strict scientific or medical model. Eating disorders have everything to do with place and space; how we take up space, how much space we take up, what encroaches on our space, how place is experienced with respect to others occupying proximate spaces, etc. Many of us complain that we often do not feel comfortable "inside our skin"—that this "continuous external contiguant" which actually separates the self from the outer domain has an awkward sensitivity . . .

Certainly there is room for the discourse of causes and effects within this model, but many observations and experiences which strain the stricter causal model are more easily accommodated here. Many of us experience body dysmorphia, for example, in connection with our eating disorders—the curious condition which refuses to allow one the privilege of experiencing or seeing one's own body as it actually is; parts or the whole often seem out of proportion or unusually large. Size and proportion, however, are fundamentally spatial. This is not to suggest, of course, that there are no causes at work in the generating of such experience. But attempting to understand body dysmorphic disorder while at the same time excluding one of its most basic features—the experience of size and proportion—would be problematic indeed.

Body dysmorphic disorder is common among us because the relation upon which it derives its manifestation—suspicion and dissatisfaction concerning one's own appearance—is a microcosm of the same suspicion and dissatisfaction we feel toward the world around us. We experience the world with its least pleasant parts inflated and emphasized. Eating disordered experience so objectifies the body-self that this same attitude is often taken towards one's own body as well; the parts whose appearance I would most like to control seem terribly to violate the parameters I would construct for them—my stomach and cheeks seem huge even when I am gaunt, the presence of any fat on my body is taken as an indicator that my whole body is becoming obese, etc. In this way, the discourse of the spatial dialectic that we have been considering makes available to us significant insights into eating disordered experiences that would, if confined to a strictly scientific model, be cut off from us and quite unexplainable.

Another problem often associated with eating disorders is the experience of great difficulties concerning matters of intimacy. Many of us simply do not experience a significant desire for emotional or sexual intimacy; some of us detest it altogether. We acknowledge our desires, but many of us seek to satisfy them (if at all) either in a solitary or a promiscuous manner rather than involving another person in an intimate or close way. We are often perceived as being emotionally withdrawn or aloof. To be sure, intimacy unavoidably involves the *proximity* of an other in both spatial and emotional contexts. In our way of thinking, which regards the world (either in part or in whole) with suspicion, we prize very much the ability to control who and what gets in and who and what stays out. This kind of attitude presents very real problems for being able to navigate intimate relationships in a good way. It would be a strain on the exclusively causal model indeed to suggest that the intimacy problems experienced by people with eating disorders were caused by past events such as sexual abuse or trauma, etc. While it may be true that a history of being abused increases one's chances for disordered eating, as a matter of fact many of us simply don't have such events in our past, but we still experience disordered eating as well as these concurrent difficulties.

Understanding eating disorders principally against the backdrop of the dialectic of the internal and the external in no way involves the rejection of a causal model of understanding. What is being offered here complements and transcends the causal model and is wholly consistent with it. If we were to look more closely at some of the current tenets of eating disorders orthodoxy that have emerged from a framework that tries to be strictly scientific, we would see the tacit use of the dialectic model here being offered. A good example of this is the current climate concerning eating disorders and genetic research.

In the present chapter, we have asserted that eating disorders affect the body but do not originate there. Specifically, the physical symptoms which affect the body are undeniable, but the disordered eating itself emerges as a function of how the space between body-self and other is navigated. Does this entail that genetics plays no role either in becoming eating disordered or in researching treatment options? Not at all. Researchers at the University of Pittsburgh (previously mentioned as conducting NIMH funded genetics investigations into anorexia) have already constructed sophisticated theories about the role of genetics in anorexic behavior. Moreover, the ideas thus far confirmed by their research make direct references to the very dialectic we have been discussing:

> It is theoretically possible that single-gene mutations might exist which result in anorexia, bulimia, or other disordered eating . . . However, it is more likely that, as with obesity, there will be multiple genes interacting with environmental variables . . . even if an individual was at high genetic risk (i.e., possessed several of these relevant genes), she might never develop anorexia nervosa if she did not live in a culture such as ours which emphasizes dieting and thinness.[2]

This is certainly an account of the development of eating disorders which draws heavily on an understanding of the relationship between something internal to the sufferer (DNA) and something external (culture). Notably, however, this scientific/genetic account of anorexia, although it sees dimly the framework we are proposing, yet still attempts to reduce it to a purely causal model—asserting ultimately that this condition is produced by genetic tendencies to react in unhealthy ways. One wonders, if the causal reduction is appropriate, then why not just as well put it in the reverse direction—that anorexia is caused by an unhealthy culture eliciting from us genetically encoded reactions? So far, the genetic research still seems to buy into the theory that disordered eating results solely from an *inner* defect:

> Once relevant genes are identified, researchers and health professionals will be able to identify high-risk individuals by their genotypes . . . Ultimately, and much further in the future, one could conceive of gene therapy to decrease or eliminate genetic risk in genetically vulnerable individuals.[3]

Insofar as eating disorders (as far as we know) are a recent development in human history whereas human DNA has remained relatively unchanged over the last several thousand years, the reverse causal proposition seems more plausible. To wit: the results of genetic research should provide grounds for "cultural therapy" rather than "gene therapy." Even the Pittsburgh researchers identify with ease some of the cultural triggers for these diseases . . . Could it be the case that eating disordered persons actually serve a useful function by helping us identify the pathological elements of our society or culture? We will explore this question further in the next chapter.

To be perfectly clear, we are not advocating the abandonment of scientific research. What seems appropriate, however, is the balancing of this perspective with one which seems to have a greater explanatory power, as well as the balancing of our results such that we become willing to make modifications on both sides of the exchange — inner and outer — personal and cultural. In the absence of this willingness to balance, the distant future spoken of by the Pittsburgh researchers will conceivably be one in which our culture is permitted to exhibit all manner of easily recognizable pathological traits (such as emphasizing dieting and thinness) that are dealt with not by tempering how we get along collectively, but rather by genetic manipulations. How this balance is best to be achieved specifically in the sciences, however, is perhaps best left to the scientist.

Radical recovery means becoming flexible with respect to the divide we create between body-self and all else. It means learning to live with a less harsh framework for interacting with the world. At the root of our unhealthy behaviors is the suspicion with which we regard the external world. When we radically recover, we learn to focus that suspicion on more appropriate elements of our experience, and we learn to translate that suspicion into more healthy behaviors. That is, we engage in behaviors that are less harmful to us and more likely to improve what we identify as wanting in our experience; we begin to interact with the world rather than withdrawing from it. We begin to take the focus off of food as an unwanted emissary, as a barrier, as an escape.

The beginning of this increase in permeability of the barrier between body-self and world is *the spoken word*. Every eating disordered person has experienced this, and it is no coincidence; the more disordered our eating becomes, the less we speak to other people. Some people say that eating disorders are "diseases of isolation," and perhaps this is why. *Radical recovery* begins with de-isolation, and this ultimately means coming out. We need to learn how to speak about our eating disorders with each other and with people who are normal eaters. Our survival ultimately depends upon our becoming able to do this. Moreover, since reconnection with the world from which we have tried to withdraw gets to the root of the problem, coming out is a more effective foundation for recovery than are other forms of treatment.

Note that the beginning of *radical recovery* is within, not without. It is we who must come out, not healthcare providers who must come in. We have already shown that to impose involuntary treatments or to cajole or to badger is to fail in the task of bringing health to us. We are afraid of you, we seek to keep you out, or at least to be able to control when you get in and when you don't, we don't like you. How will our heightened and generalized suspicions and fears be affected if you trespass on our otherwise private selves? Of course, our withdrawal will become more severe and more exaggerated, we will inevitably find our fears justified and thus we will become even sicker. This is why the treatments currently practiced are randomly efficacious at best; this is why involuntary treatments double our mortality rate.[4] We need to learn to interact in a healthy way, but this learning cannot be forced—it can only facilitated.

How do we speak about our conditions with normal eaters? Normal eaters often cannot fathom how it is possible that we can be so weird about food. Even if they say that they understand, their responses to us often betray the fact that they just don't get it at all. Those who are close to us and tolerate (or even endure) our alleged "insanity" and our failed attempts to recover a semi-normal life often exhibit a degree of patience and kindness for which they deserve sainthood. But kindness and patience in any quantity do not constitute a genuine understanding. On our side, we eating disordered tend to hear remarks spoken from a lack of understanding as careless at best and utterly disrespectful and damaging at worst. We need to learn that others have as difficult a time looking into our eating disorders from the outside as we have climbing out of them from the inside.

Many people ask what they should or can do for someone who they know or suspect is dealing with disordered eating. They want to help the person or at least refrain from doing them unintentional harm. Here is a simple answer: if I am active in my bulimia or anorexia or binge eating, there is nothing you can do to end the active phase of my disordered eating. Conversely, if I am in recovery, there is nothing you can do to make me relapse. These ideas are perhaps best treated one at a time.

First, there are many people, especially medical personnel, who reject the suggestion that they are powerless to end the active phase of disordered eating. After all, can they not force us to eat or diet? Can they not watch us and deny us access to extra food or after meal visits to the toilet? The mistake here is in thinking that proper intake of food (or keeping food down) constitutes the end of the active phase. Being bulimic or anorexic often involves a severe misery and uncomfortableness about eating or keeping food in the stomach. Being a binge eater often involves the converse misery or fear about having an empty stomach. All forms of disordered eating involve an inability to stop one's food routine and replace it with something more healthy. This misery/fear nexus associated with food, whatever its source, is not mitigated in the least by the procedure of dietary limitations, forced feeding, post-meal spying, or whatever other similar coercive procedures may be imposed upon us. In fact, these procedures may serve greatly to exacerbate the misery of eating, etc. that we so intensely experience.

Forced feedings are always inappropriate. There may be circumstances in which such excessive forms of treatment will save a greatly endangered life — but this course of action comes with a demonstrated price which is that one becomes twice as likely to die later on. For many of us bulimics and anorexics, the fear of food is strong enough that even though we know we cannot live without it, we forgo eating anyway. Treatments like forced-feeding, then, put into our bodies something that we (rationally or not) are afraid of and do not want there. So the situation is related to an issue of paternalism but seems perhaps more questionable on the grounds that it does not involve the forced intake of medicine as such, but food. Force feeding an anorexic or bulimic person will be an experience similar to a rape in that the body will be forced to accept within it what is not wanted and what is feared and what may well be very painful — it will not be experienced as a dose of good health but rather as disempowering.

If it is indeed true that eating disorders already manifest disproportionately in disempowered groups, then treatments which disempower us even more can reasonably be expected to fail. This, in our experience, is a barbaric and counter-productive method of treatment. I have been force fed and it did not help my disordered eating in the least, although I imagine it may have helped others close to me feel a bit better. Forced feeding may be a battle won, but it prolongs the war. There is no forced medical solution to disordered eating.

Second, if I am in recovery, you can't make me relapse. I often think it would be nice if everyone were considerate enough to quit offering me desserts, candies, alcohol and between meal snacks, etc. But realistically, I know that my relapses come from within. If forcing me to eat won't cure me, then likewise enticing me with food won't poison me. This takes the burden completely off those who might be inclined to tiptoe around me not wanting to leave a crumb out of place for fear that I'll eat it and be off on a week long binge and purge routine . . . And it reminds me that others are not to blame for my difficulties. Once healing begins, nothing anyone else does can prevent it. Although I'd like to blame my relapses on someone other than myself, it is not fair to do so. I won't relapse because of what you do or don't do in my presence.

That being said, those of us who are trying to recover draw strength from and very much appreciate a variety of thoughtful and kind interactions with others. The types of kindness that seem particularly helpful include refraining from trying to make us feel guilty about our disordered eating, not interpret-

ing our behavior as a deliberate attempt to hurt ourselves or others, and re-
membering that the experience of disordered eating is always more miserable
than simple observation might lead you to believe.

Of course, these are the sorts of courtesies one would hopefully grant to
any sick or otherwise debilitated person. While we may often find it tempting
to conceptualize disordered eating as some kind of moral defect or weakness
of will ("just make better choices . . ."), it is in fact a set of behaviors which
constitutes the criteria for diagnosis—and being mindful of this can be very
helpful. When I was a child, my grandmother had several strokes that left her
partially disabled on one side of her body. She was largely unable, for example, to move her left hand. It would have been utterly unhelpful (and perhaps
even harmful) if those of us who were close to her had responded to her situation by scolding her ("why can't you just move your hand?"), or by taking
her situation personally ("why are you doing this to me?"), or by otherwise
suggesting that her hand was immobile due to some defect of character that
she possessed. That someone should respond to a stroke victim in this way
seems absurd and extraordinarily callous. But if disordered eating is to be understood as a diagnosable condition, then we should not respond to disordered
eating in such fashion either. When my eating is disordered, my eating normally is as much something I can choose to do as fully utilizing her left hand
was something my grandmother could have chosen to do. No process of de-
liberation and choice that is familiar to me could have moved my grandmother's hand or made a normal eater out of me.

And yet, my grandmother regained much of the mobility in her hand, and
I have been eating in a healthy way for more than seven years at the time of
this writing. The notion that disordered eating is an illness constituted by specific behaviors accomplishes much in the way of clearing some room for *radical recovery*. It may preclude our chastising people who suffer, but it also
opens up other more effective and compassionate possibilities for responding
to this virulent and deadly form of suffering. I have spoken with literally hundreds of other people who have been in all stages of suffering and recovery,
and our experiences unanimously confirm that disordered eating cannot possibly be affected in any positive way by nagging, cajoling, badgering, scolding, shaming, force-feeding, or any other form of interaction that is anything
less than compassionate.

This is not to suggest that the principal burden for any one person's recovery rests with the conduct of someone else. At the same time, however, it is
possible—in the absence of compassion and understanding—to impede
someone's recovery, even unintentionally. So what is the answer? What is the
solution to the problem? The whole thrust of this book has been to advance

the truth that *manifesto* is our *radical recovery*. Coming out cannot be forced, but it can be facilitated. It cannot be demanded, but it can be accepted. It may not be understood, but it can help heal anyway.

Current strategies for understanding and dealing with disordered eating are such that few people are significantly helped, most people don't get better. Since the current strategies are not sufficient for our healing, we need something *radical*. This book is part of my *radical recovery*. In reading it and sharing it, it becomes part of your *radical recovery*. This book is part of my breach of the divide between you and me. I hope that you will receive it in a good way, with an open mind and a willingness to give further examination to what others say about their eating disorders. I hope that you will, in turn, share this breach with another person. If you do not receive this in a good way, however, if you find it trivial or incorrect or self indulgent or too unscientific to be of value, that's fine too. *Radical recovery* is, after all, *radical*, and we radicals are not thwarted by the mere fact that some people want to stick with old ways of dealing with problems even though they have been proven not to work.

If you are an eating disordered reader, I especially thank you for reading this book; in doing so you have permitted me to share something with you. The disordered eating that we experience is rooted in separation. That means that our healing lies in coming together, and in these pages we have begun that task of reaching out. From where ever I am at this moment to where ever you are at this moment, I embrace you and I wish you well. Now please come out with me, *out needs company*.

NOTES

1. See especially Carol Gilligan, *In A Different Voice: Psychological Theory and Women's Development* (Cambridge, MA: Harvard University Press, 1982).

2. University of Pittsburg Department of Psychiatry, "Brave New World: The Role of Genetics in Prevention and Treatment of Eating Disorders," *A Collaborative Study of the Genetics of Anorexia Nervosa and Bulimia Nervosa*, <http://www.wpic.pitt.edu/research/pfanbn/genetics.html>

3. University of Pittsburg Department of Psychiatry, "Brave New World."

4. Ramsay, R., A. Ward, J. Treasure, and G.F. Russell, "Compulsory Treatment in Anorexia Nervosa. Short-Term Benefits and Long-Term Mortality," *British Journal of Psychiatry* 175 (1999): 147–53.

Chapter Five

ED Pride: Disorder Without Disease

It has been suggested in previous chapters that one can find a significant sense of pride in the fact that one is eating disordered. Many readers will no doubt be wondering how it is that a condition that has been repeatedly portrayed in these pages as one of the most widespread, deadly and yet ignored epidemics could possibly be something about which one is proud. There is, however, a cogent explanation for the pride that many eating disordered people are beginning to express. It is the task of this chapter to give an account of this pride and the movement in which it's expression has begun, as well as to promote it and to defend it against it's critics and detractors.

We have found that the discourse of a dialectic of internal and external is most helpful indeed in articulating the phenomenology of eating disordered experience. It became clear in the analysis offered in the previous chapter that the scientific causal model for explaining eating disorders was lacking some important features that were supplied by including, along side that linear temporal account, a spatial understanding of eating disordered experience. To be sure, we do not mean to assert that what is external is entirely separate and distinct from what is internal. The *relationship* between these domains is precisely what is at the heart of being eating disordered; the disorder emerges and recedes according to how one navigates and experiences the space between body-self and other.

We are certainly able to refer to these internal and external domains in a coherent and responsible way without postulating their independence from one another. Moreover, we have shown that it is useful and productive to do so insofar as this discourse provides insights into our conditions that would otherwise remain unavailable. This discourse is useful, however, in another important way as well; it makes possible an articulation of eating disorder pride. Such an articulation involves the following simple use of terms which have

already been employed in this book. Let "disordered eating" refer to those behaviors which form the diagnostic criteria given in the DSM-IV. Conversely,
let "eating disordered" refer to the psychological or conceptual framework
(brought to light in the previous chapter) which seeks to erect boundaries that
mark off the self from an environment that is regarded with an attitude of suspicion or fear. In this way, we have transferred our useful terms from the last
chapter to the present; "disordered eating" referring to behavior that is accessible to an external observer, "eating disordered" referring to the internal
mental states from which the behavior has emerged.

Similarly, we can acknowledge that there is a relation between these domains of inward ideas and outward behaviors without conflating them. Although one's ideas are not the same as one's actions, ideas and actions very
often exert a mutual influence upon one another. Much of this mutual influence has been more expertly articulated by others who specialize in behavioral psychology or the philosophy of mind; the focus of this chapter would
be lost if we were to attempt to cover that terrain here. It should be sufficient
to the academic reader as well as to those readers interested in eating disorders simply to point out that ideas often form the basis for actions, and actions
often give rise to and reinforce certain ideas. My eating disorder and my disordered eating, then, are related to one another but they are not identical.
Which of these interrelated domains, the internal way of interpreting one's relation to one's environment, or the external observable interaction with one's
environment, constitutes the "illnesses" that we have been discussing?

The single most important idea at stake in eating disorder pride is this: *eating disorders as such do not constitute a disease or an illness.* One can be
quite eating disordered in one's psychological constitution and yet eat in a
non-disordered fashion. Treatment providers have plenty to say about the relation between our thinking and the unhealthy behaviors that can result from
it. There is much to be said, however, of the distinction between being eating
disordered and suffering from disordered eating—and it is vitally important,
especially from the standpoint of treatment, to speak of this distinction—it is
not a mere game with words. It may well be the case that disordered eating
behavior arises principally from inward experience that is eating disordered,
but it is certainly possible to have this inward experience and yet eat in a
healthy and relatively "normal" way. The condition which we are describing
is commonly called "recovery."

Although recovery has been shown not to be the norm for us, the reason
why this is so has also shown itself; the likelihood of recovery is minimized
when prevalence is not acknowledged—research is not conducted, and treatment options are unreliable. Even the most pessimistic portrayal of the cur-

rent climate in healthcare opportunities, however, must allow for at least the possibility of recovery. That is, it is at least a coherent idea to suppose that someone experiences all of the inward psychological features of eating disordered life as we have described it and yet exists in a relative state of recovery. This author is, in fact, currently existing in such a state, as are other people with whom I am acquainted.

But if we concede the intelligibility of being both eating disordered and in recovery, as surely we must because it is an actuality for a small but fortunate percentage of us, then we have already made the distinction between having an eating disorder and having disordered eating. I consider myself to be quite severely eating disordered, but I am not sick, or diseased, or ill. I understand that my eating disorders can manifest themselves in some very unhealthy and potentially deadly behaviors, but they are not doing so at present. *The sickness, therefore, resides solely in the behaviors that form the basis for diagnosis.*

Apart from the observable behavior of disordered eating, there are very few criteria for making a diagnosis. The only diagnostic criteria that are psychological rather than behavioral involve attitudes about body weight that are associated with anorexia and bulimia. "Fear of gaining weight, denial of seriousness of low body weight, and undue influence of body shape on self-evaluation" are psychological features which form part of the DSM-IV criteria for diagnosing anorexia. In diagnosing bulimia, all criteria are behavioral except "undue influence of body shape on self-evaluation and a sense of lack of control over eating." Moreover, the DSM-IV appears excessive in this regard, as other diagnostic manuals either do not include any psychological criteria or include far less than the DSM-IV. The ICD-10, for example, mentions that eating disorders are often "associated with a specific psychopathology," but does not present any psychological features as diagnostic. The NHS Primary Care Protocols mentions only "morbid dread of fatness" in connection with anorexia and bulimia.

It is also worth noting that until recently in the history of diagnosing disordered eating, psychological features were not part of any diagnostic criteria— diagnostic criteria were entirely behavioral until the latter half of the twentieth century. There has been considerable speculation as to precisely when and why physicians began to enumerate their anorexic and bulimic patients' "dread of fatness," etc. The general consensus seems to be that these psychological features became apparent in the latter half of the nineteenth century, and that prior to this time the principal motivations for restrictive eating behaviors were religious in nature.[1]

Although the presence of psychological factors such as weight phobia in the diagnostic criteria has spurred recent debate, the issue need not detract from our claim here that disordered eating is constituted solely by unhealthy behaviors. The reason we can maintain this claim despite diagnostic criteria that are obviously psychological rather than behavioral is that the psychological criteria are neither necessary nor sufficient for diagnosis. Since we anorexics and bulimics often deny being weight phobic, and since such a phobia might find verbal expression in any number of other modes of discourse (depending on the cultural, religious, and psychological familiarities of the "patient"), we are in fact able to diagnose anorexia and bulimia without any direct evidence of weight phobia. Specific motive is not a necessity.

Neither are psychological states sufficient for diagnosing disordered eating. Weight phobia would be meaningless as a criterion for diagnosing anything in a person who exhibited no disordered behaviors. In fact, such factors as weight phobia only seem useful at all when the person who has such a fear is already known to have disordered eating. In the absence of the behavioral aspects of disordered eating, the presence of weight phobia indicates nothing.

It has been explained that eating disordered experience, thought and feeling provide a basic framework from which disordered behavior may arise. The diagnostic criteria, however, are not used to discern the presence of this framework of experiences that we call "eating disorder." The diagnostic criteria are used to discern the presence of behaviors that constitute "disordered eating." Even though some of the criteria are psychological, their clear intent is to help us distinguish between unhealthy eating that is "disordered" and unhealthy eating that is attributable to some other medical explanation. These criteria, although apparently psychological, have the specific purpose of distinguishing between different behaviors.

Regardless of what one thinks or feels or experiences, one must be engaged in a specified set of actions in order to be diagnosed. Since the diagnostic criteria have this purely behavioral orientation, we are able to conclude that being inwardly eating disordered—*by itself*—cannot be construed as in any way unhealthy or bad. Being eating disordered involves having a certain kind of perspective on the world, a framework for appropriating and experiencing and navigating the world according to a certain way of thinking which I've tried to articulate in the previous chapter. The inadequacies of my account will have to be brought to light and amended by other eating disordered individuals, and I will gladly take their advice to heart on this matter. To suffer from disordered eating, however, requires very little articulation or elaboration—all such details are given in the DSM-IV diagnostic criteria.

We observe that inwardly eating disordered people are far more likely perhaps to develop disordered eating behaviors, but what follows from this? Certainly nothing about whether it's a good or bad thing to be inwardly eating disordered. It is commonly noted that women suffer from disordered eating significantly more than men, but we do not take this as evidence that there is something unhealthy or inappropriate about being female. It often happens that one group of people is more likely to be diagnosed with an illness or disease than another, but it never follows from this that being part of that group itself constitutes a disease. Even when an identifiable disease affects only one group of people, we still do not conflate the group that gets the disease with the notion of disease itself. Only persons of African ancestry get sickle-cell anemia, but it would be ridiculous indeed to suggest that having African ancestry is therefore a disease. Similarly, it may well be the case that only people who think and feel in an eating disordered way end up with disordered eating behaviors, but this does not mean that there's anything unhealthy or wrong with such thinking and feeling. To be sure, disordered eating is unhealthy and requires treatment in order to be arrested such that the health of the body can be insured. Being eating disordered, however, does not constitute any form of illness or disease.

For all of the reasons previously discussed in this book, it is best consistently to advocate for adequate research and treatment for people with disordered eating. Anything less than this constitutes an inadequate and inexcusable response to the fact of epidemic disordered eating in the United States. But how should we respond to the psychological disposition which often gives rise to disordered eating? Should we try to reduce the prevalence of disordered eating behaviors by alleging that such psychological constitutions which give rise to them are defective, and then attempt to replace or restructure these psyches with a variety of therapies, drugs, and other treatments? Or would it be better to affirm a person's inner most structure of self and then assist them in manifesting that self in the world in a way that is conducive to physical health? The moral implications involved in making such judgments are obviously far reaching. And yet, without questioning the appropriateness of this precarious inference, modern medicine has consistently chosen to treat our minds as though they were as diseased as our behaviors.

It is interesting indeed that no one has seriously posed these questions to the authorities within eating disorders orthodoxy. What is implied by the fact that eating disorders are considered *mental* illnesses, and yet they are diagnosed solely on the basis of *behaviors*? Without acknowledging that there might be something amiss in equating a person's inner mental states with a person's outward observable behavior, eating disorders orthodoxy has applied the judgment "diseased" to our behavior, and then clandestinely transferred this judgment wholesale to our psychological makeup. The result has been that treatment options are very one-sided indeed, acknowledging our inward dispositions only insofar as they need to be changed while ignoring the possibility of affirming our "take" on life and teaching us how to live with it in a good way. The CDC's advice that disordered eating is the result of poor choices is offensive precisely because it conflates outward behavior with inward state of mind, and then takes the disease of the former as evidence that the latter is defective.

How do we know that the inward conceptual framework of the eating disordered person is not exactly as it ought to be? How do we know that the problem doesn't reside in being provided a *defective environment* in which one's natural psychological constitution might otherwise flourish? Not only do we need to ask these questions, but in light of the fact that these illnesses are behavioral, we need to insist that who we are does not need to be changed. We obviously need to change the ways that we cope with the world and interact with food, but these behaviors can more effectively be improved by affirming who we are in a positive way than by the simplistic and obviously fallacious reasoning offered by the CDC and others.

Locked into their linear cause and effect model of explanation, therapists and other alleged experts often tell us that disordered eating is a product of low self esteem. After convincing us of this, however, we are told that we are defective in the ways that we think about the world, relationships, and food. How is our esteem supposed to be improved by convincing us that we are defective? Is it not much more likely that our understanding of self will be bolstered by acknowledging who we are as fundamentally good and proper? The best conditions for the possibility of recovery depend upon coming to believe this important truth: *we do not need to change who we are, we need to change what we do.* In regard to our outward behavior, the defect is obvious enough— disordered eating constitutes the tenth leading cause of death in the United States. Regarding our inward selves, however, the notion of defect must be replaced by pride. This, of course, raises a significant question: if I know that my inward psychological constitution makes me more likely to manifest disordered eating, why be proud of my inward psychological constitution? The answer to this question has already been suggested, it only needs to be made explicit.

Since being eating disordered itself does not constitute a sickness or a disease, it certainly can be regarded in a positive light. Being proud of who we are can be justified by further explicating the inward psychological perspective which we examined in the previous chapter. Specifically, we noted that restrictive eating disordered behavior (anorexia and bulimia) involves an over-focusing on food such that food receives the brunt of our suspicions and fears about the world around us. We transfer that fear and suspicion to food because it is easier to manage. There are many undesirable and fearsome features of the external world that I cannot control in the least, but I can control what I eat or don't eat, even to the extreme of starving and/or purging. I therefore let the food stand in as a representative of those features of the world I would resist or change or control, and my feelings of fear and suspicion are mitigated—I am once again able to function in a world that is threatening. As well, as a binge eater I am much more comfortable relating to food than I am relating to other people because people are perceived as fearsome or intimidating. Whatever my reason for feeling so uncomfortable in the web of human relationships, my ability to function in those entanglements—even with people who are grossly undesirable to me—is restored once I can keep them at a safe distance. Food accomplishes this insofar as it functions as a surrogate other, and insofar as over-consuming it adds a physical barrier to my body. I have heard many overweight people and many underweight people express the sentiment that one of the benefits of being too big or too small is that others cease regarding you as a potential romantic, sexual, or social interest, or that others lose their interest in relating to you at all. Some people take objection to this loss of interest based on body-type, and appropriately so, but they are expressing pride when they so take objection; who I am is more important than what I look like.

The point here is not to reduce all disordered eating to a single cause, and the point is certainly not to make an attempt to speak the inner thoughts of all eating disordered people. The point is to take note that whatever our specific inner thoughts and feelings are, they are very often colored with this propensity to find that the world around us—for whatever reason(s)—deserves to be regarded with great caution, perhaps even suspicion and fear, and maybe even resisted altogether. Since it is very difficult indeed to function in a world that is regarded in this way, we let food stand in and "take the blame."

In my own case, and upon careful and lengthy reflection, I have become aware of numerous critical observations of my social, political, moral, and religious environment that have been dealt with in this fashion. I find it most disagreeable and upsetting, for example, that our society has been built upon the practice of discrimination, and continues to discriminate. Racial minorities, women, gays, and non-Christians have consistently been marginalized in my culture and they have suffered much identifiable harm as a result. I don't want to be part of that juggernaut of social and political injustice. Many people in my culture seem to have at least some awareness that the United States was constructed (at least in part) by virtue of an extraordinary genocide in which more than 95 percent of the original Native Peoples of the continent were systematically exterminated by "settlers." Despite this vague awareness, however, few people bother to talk about it, many people think I'm crazy for harping on it so much, and nearly everyone seems to think that it is too late to do anything about it. I don't want to be part of a "civilization" that was constructed over top of the dead bodies of an entire race. In similar fashion, I have severe misgivings about the technologizing, televising, uranium-mining, earth-ruining, carcinogen advocating, profit and war mongering capitalistic propensities of the Euro-American culture that has taken over the continent on which I live!

Absolutely, without question, many eating disordered readers will have no inclination whatsoever to agree with me on any of these points. But, I bet each of you could come up with a list of *your own* that expresses dissatisfactions, misgivings, harsh criticisms, fears, or suspicions about the current state of affairs if you spent some time thinking it over. You might not focus on issues of moral and political import, perhaps you are reading this from an entirely different cultural perspective. Maybe your environment is dominated by a few individuals rather than an identifiable class or group against whom you engage in some mental or physical resistance. The possibilities for variety in *content* are endless here, but there is a common *form* of thinking which—as we have already described it—marks off some aspect of the external world for the purpose of protection, safety, or comfort. Such desired comfort may be political in orientation, it may be religious, or physical, or familial, or it may be more generalized. But we seek comfort in our disordered eating behaviors, and that means that we find discomfort in some aspect of our environment.

Now, in carefully considering any of these identifiable or specifiable elements of the external world that give rise to this feeling of discomfort, one realizes that in fact one is able to discern *something* about the world that needs to be drawn into question or subjected to some kind of evaluation and scrutiny. Were this not so, the discomfort would never arise, nor would we feel the need to deal with it in such a harsh manner. The fact of the matter is this: *we eating disordered people are gifted with a sensitivity to our environment that not everyone seems to possess*. We notice on a most basic and intuitive level what others often fail to notice even after having it pointed out to them—that there are facets of this world such as society, culture, political economic system, environment, family, etc.—that need to be drawn into question and subjected to some kind of scrutiny, and may even be such that they are unacceptable and should be resisted, withdrawn from, feared, kept out . . . Perhaps each of us identifies different specific features that we feel meet this description, but in this regard we differ only in the content of our thinking; we share a form of mental outlook or psychological disposition and constitution.

There are some who would suggest that life is actually better when one is unable clearly to discern the features of one's world that are in dire need of change. These are the people who would treat us by reshaping our inward experience of the world, transforming us into people who don't take things so seriously or perhaps come to think of the ability to discern what needs to be improved as a defect of character. They may indeed find life more pleasant when it involves a naïve acceptance of this kind, but they only know their own side of things.

Although one might rightly be cautious about adopting a wholly utilitarian moral outlook, there are some significant psychological insights offered in this regard by one of the best known proponents of utilitarian ethics—John Stuart Mill. Of interest here is Mill's argument that in order to be a competent judge between alternative ways of living or understanding, one would have to have experience of both. If only one way of life is experienced but not the other, then one has no real basis for comparing the two. Regarding such comparisons, Mill puts it this way:

> If one of the two is, by those who are competently acquainted with both, placed so far above the other that they prefer it, even though knowing it to be attended with a greater amount of discontent, and would not resign it for any quantity of the other pleasure which their nature is capable of, we are justified in ascribing to the preferred enjoyment a superiority in quality, so far outweighing quantity as to render it, in comparison, of small account.[2]

So how about it? Would you rather have some significant insights as to how the world (or maybe just your particular corner of it) needs to be changed, what works and what doesn't, what's good and what's not so good? Or would you prefer an existence in which you have few or no sensitivities to such matters? Supposing that both states could be equally conjoined with good health, which would you choose? You—eating disordered reader—are a "competent judge." My own inclination is to agree with Mill's subsequent comments on these matters in which he offers an eloquent account of the bases for human dignity and pride. Please read the following important passage, also from *Utilitarianism*, not so much as an endorsement of Mill's ethics, but rather as an explication of the psychology of pride and dignity, especially as it applies to we who are eating disordered. We can recognize the necessity of changing our outward coping behaviors, while at the same time maintaining a sense of pride in who we are and especially the sensitivities that, although varying a great deal in their content, seem to be significantly more developed in us than they are in the general population:

> [N]o intelligent human being would consent to be a fool, no instructed person would be an ignoramus, no person of feeling and conscience would be selfish and base, even though they should be persuaded that the fool, the dunce, or the rascal is better satisfied with his lot than they are with theirs . . . We may give

what explanation we please of this unwillingness; we may attribute it to pride, . . . but its most appropriate appellation is a sense of dignity, which all human beings possess in one form or other . . .[3]

I do not want treatment that makes my recovery dependant upon abdicating those faculties which are good and useful, simply because I have not learned to cope with the feelings which result from those faculties. I want to keep my insights and intuitions about the world, and yet navigate the world and interact with it in a healthy way. Recovery has, for us, in the history of treating disordered eating, not involved this affirming perspective on the mental framework that we already possess.

Radical recovery includes a radical sense of pride which affirms the self in-itself. Eating disorder pride does not affirm the self at the expense of others or in a comparative or derogatory way. The pride we have in mind here acknowledges that even when my eating is severely disordered, it is more healthy for me to affirm who I am than it is for me to think that my unhealthy outward behavior indicates an inner defect.

It is vitally important that people with our way of looking at the world exist. Without us, that is without people insightful and courageous enough to refuse to trade in our warranted dissatisfactions, the likelihood that the world's multitude of problems will come to light and be dealt with in a productive way is seriously diminished. In this way, we might come to see ourselves as something akin to the miner's canary. Sent into the mine, the canary's survival indicated breathable air, and therefore safety for the miner. Without the canary, the miner's survival depended on luck, chance, and good fortune.

The researchers at the University of Pittsburgh who are studying the genetic components of anorexia have recognized the similar role of anorexics, but only dimly. They have identified, by virtue of its ill effects on some women, a pathological trait of our culture: "she might never develop anorexia nervosa if she did not live in a culture such as ours which emphasizes dieting and thinness."[4] As mentioned in the previous chapter, there are two different directions in which one could proceed with this observation. The first is the direction suggested by the Pittsburgh research team, and it is wholly consistent with the dominant medical perspective on treatment for disordered eating: "one could conceive of gene therapy to decrease or eliminate genetic risk in genetically vulnerable individuals."[5] That is, we understand anorexia to be a response to external stimuli, and we treat the anorexia by changing the individual so that she no longer responds to these stimuli in the same way. But it does not occur to these researchers that it may be better to proceed in the other direction. Perhaps we should thank the anorexic for responding as she does, if for no other reason than that she has awakened our insights concerning a specific feature of our culture that is unhealthy? When these researchers identify "emphasis on dieting and thinness" as a triggering mechanism for anorexic behavior, they are basically telling us that our culture's idea of what constitutes ideal body image is a *psychological carcinogen*.

We very much need to be made aware of the carcinogenic elements of our environment, whether they are physical or psychological. If some feature of our culture is so concretely identified as having this effect on a significant number of women, then we need to rethink our culture—not our women. How would things stand if, after identifying the carcinogens contained in cigarettes, we encouraged smokers to keep smoking because we were going to treat them by manipulating their genes so that they wouldn't respond to cigarettes in an unhealthy way? One could imagine a culture that engaged in genetic manipulations *ad infinitum* as a perpetual attempt to eliminate all unhealthy responses to the physical and social environment, while at the same time never calling into question the practicality or morality of such a framework for treatment. Sooner or later it must occur to us that what needs to be manipulated is not *within* the person being treated but *without*.

The miner who attempts to breed canaries that can survive excessive levels of carbon monoxide is certainly insane. Is it not in the miner's best interest to keep the canaries that respond naturally and change the quality of the air instead? In like fashion, the vast and overwhelming prevalence of disordered eating is an indication that something is seriously wrong with our culture. We may speculate and debate about exactly what the problems are, but the fact is that we are reacting to pathological elements of our environment. As such, our disordered eating reflects a mental framework of sensitivities for which our culture should be grateful. This gratitude needs to be demanded by us. We demand it by speaking out loud about our eating disorders and telling people that we are proud of who we are, that we have some useful ideas about improving the social environment in which we live, and that we are not so much "ill" as we are particularly sensitive to the sickness-inducing features of our world.

The canary is not superior to the miner, and we are not superior to any of our fellow humans. The canary has a sensitivity, and we evidently have sensitivities to a certain degree that other humans do not. But what affects us adversely may certainly have adverse effects on others who don't respond the same way we do, just as what kills the canary will eventually kill the miner. This places some responsibility on us as well as those who are in positions of authority in eating disorders orthodoxy. It is not only in our own best interest to adopt an attitude of ED Pride, but it may be in the best interest of others as well.

Emphasis on dieting and thinness, ability to consume as a financial indicator of status, buffets and fast food restaurants on every street corner, casket companies that make "super-size" caskets, etc., are all symptoms of some cultural condition that very much wants to be noticed. A significant percentage of the world's population doesn't have enough to eat, and yet in the United States disordered eating is epidemic. Is the problem in the impoverished countries? Or is it the United States that has lost control of its cultural understanding of consumption and mindfulness of others? The fact that we'd rather genetically mutate our own people than even so much as acknowledge these questions speaks volumes indeed.

We have given much attention to the manner in which our healthcare system turns a blind eye to disordered eating; eating disorders remain minimally researched, and there is no accepted model for treatment despite prevalence and mortality information which suggests a crisis of epidemic proportions. Our culture turns a blind eye in a more general way, and we can see this quite clearly reflected in the attitudes and assumptions which form the background for our medical understanding of issues related to weight and the consumption of food. Particularly revealing in this regard is the recent *JAMA* article to which we devoted significant discussion in the first three chapters.

This study, it will be recalled, sought to correlate mortality with three distinct weight groups; underweight, overweight, and obese. The results of this study were interesting indeed. As we have already noted, this study indicated that there were about 112,000 more deaths than expected in 2000 among obese individuals, and 34,000 more deaths than expected among underweight individuals.[6] Curiously, this study found that about 86,000 *fewer* deaths than expected were associated with being overweight.

Thus far our analysis has focused on the excess deaths associated with being "obese" or "underweight." But what should we make of the 86,000 fewer deaths than expected in the "overweight" group? Does this indicate that being overweight is *more healthy* than not being overweight? The authors of this article appear to have no answer to this question, as they have devoted little discussion to this portion of the data. One would expect, at the very least, that such an obviously anomalous finding would be acknowledged somewhere in the medical community's appropriation of this data. Meaningful inquiry as to the meaning of finding the fewest excess deaths in the "overweight" category, however, has not occurred.

The federal guidelines for distinguishing between the different weight categories used for this study are based on body mass index (BMI).[7] Table 5.1 indicates the categories which inform the study under consideration.[8]

Table 5.1. Excess Deaths by Weight (BMI), According to
Flegal, Graubard, Williamson, and Gail, (2005)

BMI	Weight Status	Excess Deaths
Below 18.5	Underweight	33,746
18.5–24.9	Normal	0
25.0–29.9	Overweight	−86,094
30.0 and above	Obese	111,909

In this study, the authors calculated how many deaths were "expected" in a weight (BMI) range by considering the "normal" category as the standard or "reference BMI category."[9] The authors do not state, however, why they chose to use the "normal" weight category as the standard or baseline for this comparison. Although noting that federal guidelines define weight ranges according to table 5.1, this study fails to indicate any precise justification for privileging one of these ranges by regarding it as a standard for comparison. Curiously, the federal guidelines cited as definitive regarding weight ranges are in direct conflict with the results offered in this study, as the guidelines clearly state that "overweight substantially increase[s] the risk of morbidity."[10] The authors of this study therefore appear to have missed an obvious opportunity to draw into question the federal guidelines for the definition of what constitutes "normal" weight.

This study indicates that more than 40 percent of the population is in the "normal" (BMI 18.5–24.9) range, and that this is more than the percentage of the population that is in any of the other ranges.[11] Other than this, however, there is no reason indicated for the baseline status of the "normal" weight group. Is prevalence a sufficient reason for labeling a weight range "normal?" Or should something else be the principal criterion for this distinction?

In terms of the mere presentation of data resulting from this study, it is obvious that any of the weight (BMI) ranges could have been chosen as the baseline or point of reference for these comparisons. It should also be obvious that the most reasonable baseline or reference range would be the range which showed the fewest number of excess deaths. Since the study purports to examine *excess* deaths, and all other ranges have deaths *in excess* of the range with the fewest excess deaths, the range with the fewest excess deaths most reasonably constitutes the reference or standard for these comparisons. Left in its original interpretation, the data suggest that the "overweight" (25.0–29.9 BMI) range is associated with *negative excess deaths*. Has no one thought to ask just how it is that we are to understand the meaning of a *negative excess*?

"Normal" is a label which is presumably intended to suggest a weight (or BMI) that is "optimal" or most desirable. But that which is "optimal" should be that which is most conducive to a long and healthy life. The data from this study strongly suggest that the "overweight" range is more desirable than any other for the simple reason that this range was associated with fewest number of excess deaths. This range should therefore receive the label "optimal" and should constitute our point of reference for these comparisons.

The fact that we presently understand "normal weight" in terms of a BMI range that is not "optimal" suggests two important insights. In the first place, it indicates that we are largely ignorant of what constitutes a healthy weight; we are willing to acknowledge as normal what is clearly unhealthy, and we do not formally recognize any kind of obesity as indicative of problematic eating. Secondly, this indicates that both the prevalence of disordered eating and the number of deaths associated with being outside the parameters of optimal weight are likely to be significantly higher than what we estimated in the first chapter, even though that estimate was enormous. We can speculate that prevalence and mortality are far greater than our initial estimates because the weight categories that underlie all such estimates at present are severely skewed in a way which obscures our ability to recognize unhealthy weight.

If the healthiest weight range (rather than the most popular one) were used as the baseline or point of reference with an excess death estimate of zero, and the excess deaths from this study adjusted so as to reflect their relation to the genuinely optimal weight category, our table would look quite different indeed. In effect, we would have to add roughly 86,000 excess deaths to each of the other categories to find out their status relative to the optimal (BMI 25.0–29.9) range. Since it is more reasonable to think that the healthiest range should constitute this baseline, table 5.2 is a more responsible interpretation of the precise numbers from this same study.

From this it follows that 489,651 deaths annually are associated with being outside the parameters of optimal weight (or BMI). This makes our earlier claim that eating disorders constitute the tenth leading cause of death in the United States seem conservative indeed. If even half of these deaths were understood to be a reflection of disordered eating in the United States, then disordered eating would in fact constitute the third leading cause of death among Americans.[12]

Table 5.2. Excess Deaths by Weight (BMI), Revised

BMI	Weight Status	Excess Deaths
Below 18.5	Severely Underweight	119,840
18.5–24.9	Underweight	86,094
25.0–29.9	Optimal	0
30.0–34.9	Overweight	115,557
35 and above	Severely Overweight	168,160

As a culture, we call a weight range demonstrated to be unhealthy (because it is too low) "normal." As a culture, we seem to be sharing a collective experience of anorexia; "refusal to maintain body weight at or above a minimally normal weight for age and height . . ."[13]

When you think about it, our culture is bulimic as well, and even meets all the diagnostic criteria that would be necessary for such a claim. As already noted, we spend more than $100 billion per year on fast food.[14] If our spending indicates our priorities, we value our trips to McDonald's more than the vehicles we use to get there, more than the computers we allegedly need for everyday life, and more than our kids' educations. As far as what we spend, all these other items take a back seat. It is as though we take fast food to be a necessity, whereas cars, computers, and education are luxuries. Not only do we go to these extreme lengths to over-consume, but we evidently feel so guilty afterward that we engage in "compensatory spending" and sink nearly $50 billion per year into diet and weight loss programs.

If an individual were to engage in this behavior; rapid consumption to the point of near bursting followed by compensatory behavior such as purging, starving or excessive exercise, that individual would merit a diagnosis of bulimia. How is it that our culture can engage in this behavior on such an enormous and grotesque scale, and escape the same diagnosis? Moreover, why are people surprised that there are so many bulimics in our culture? Shouldn't it be more of a shock to find that there are so many non-bulimics living in a fundamentally bulimic society? If you wanted to design a culture with the specific and perverse goal of producing a significant number of citizens with disordered eating, wouldn't this be it?

Again, rather than ask these basic and telling questions and subjecting to scrutiny our understanding of what constitutes healthy weight, the orthodoxy responsible for our health finds it a better alternative to suggest genetic mutation and making "better choices." We eating disordered, however, are going to ask these questions until we get answers. Our silence is obviously more desirable to some, since we are often ignored, minimized, or used as material for the entertainment of the general public. But we must not comply with this. We must not internalize this defective cultural understanding of "normal" weight, and we must not internalize the shame and denial with which most of our fellow creatures regard disordered eating. We must not submit to our culture's subtle attempts to disguise our prevalence and even our very existence. We must be proud of who we are, we must be proud that we actually respond to an unhealthy environment in a way which is wholly deserved and called for. *Psychological "disorder" exists, if at all, in the medical attitudes that would seek to convince the general public (by way of a clever presentation of numbers) that "normal" weight is best understood as a range in which we see 86,000 excess deaths per year.*

You know why we are referred to as "disordered?" It is not because there's something actually wrong with us, we respond to an insane culture the way you would expect any sane creature to respond. Although our culture is immensely insane when it comes to issues of weight, food and consumption, it is nonetheless *orderly*. Our presence threatens to disrupt the order and predictability of the insanity to which we have become accustomed. We are, therefore, "disordered" because we count as positive evidence for changing the way our culture relates to food and other matters of consumption. What could be a more tangible source of pride than to be living evidence that points society in a better direction?

Some readers may find these statements of pride to be exaggerated or overstated. In fact, they are simply long over-due. Mill's point is well taken in this regard. Which seems preferable: to be a sane individual in an insane culture, or to be an insane individual in a sane culture? Of course, the best alternative would be personal sanity in a sane culture. The former of these two, however, would be preferable to the latter for anyone with experience of both sanity and insanity. If one is sane in an insane culture, one will of course be judged as insane simply because one deviates from some accepted set of norms—but one wouldn't *really* be insane. "Sane" and "insane" are labels which are at least as much a reflection of socially constructed norms as of internal mental goings on.

Most of us who have begun openly to express our pride have been ignored, some of us have been ridiculed, and a few of us have even been vilified and greatly feared. Although this last statement may appear extreme, it is shown to be true by way of examining the recent responses to certain internet sites that have been labeled "pro-anorexia" or "pro-bulimia." The prefix "pro" has been used in connection with these web-sites in order to suggest that they promote disordered eating. The usual format for such web-sites is that people post messages to one another about their disordered eating; they share information and support, and sometimes the shared information is specifically about how to be more efficient (or perhaps less likely to be discovered) in one's disordered eating behavior.

The alternative to these "pro-ana" and "pro-mia" (i.e.—pro-anorexia and pro-bulimia) sites is comprised mainly of sites that are labeled "pro-recovery." The pro-recovery sites are not at all controversial, since they seem largely to buy into the notion that eating disorders are diseases of the mind that find expression in one's behavior. Many of these pro-recovery sites are very helpful indeed, providing information about treatment providers, support groups, literature, and information for friends and family. Some of these pro-recovery sites have won awards for their careful attention to these matters, and deservedly so. The pro-ana and pro-mia sites, however, have received a very different response indeed. For the most part, they have been demonized as dangerous and inappropriate promoters of unhealthy behaviors, and many of them have been shut down as a result of this public outcry. Here are some typical comments about pro-ana and pro-mia web-sites. The first is from Anorexia Truth:

> Why would someone be so sick of mind to try to encourage others to starve themselves to death? Many web hosting companies have now banned these sites, and so some search engines will not find many Pro-Anna [sic] sites.[15]

This one is from Preteenagers Today:

> Currently, an alarming number of pro-anorexia web sites are popping up on the Internet. Despite a recent ban by several of the larger search engines, there has still been a steady onslaught of sites continuing to surface on the Internet. These sites are extremely harmful to impressionable young people, often promoting anorexia as a lifestyle rather than a serious disease.[16]

Finally, here's one from The Washington Post:

> Despite attempts to encourage internet service providers to close down such sites, many continue to exist. A recent Google search using the term "pro-anorexia" yielded 30,000-plus results. Many were links to pages by health authorities warning about the pro-anorexia movement . . . Carol Day, director of health education services at Georgetown University and a member of the school's eating disorder treatment team, called the sites "dangerous and disturbing." Experts say the sites can reinforce unhealthy behaviors, slow the recovery process and discourage people from seeking help. "I think anyone who is working in the field of eating disorders realizes how unhealthy" the sites are, Day said.[17]

Such a list of quotations could go on at great length with little variation. The consensus among the "experts" seems unanimous in asserting that the "pro-anorexia movement" promotes an unhealthy lifestyle and is therefore "dangerous and disturbing." In making such statements, the "experts" have taken what is arguably the only real expression of pride that has emerged strictly from within the ED community and they have proclaimed it as evil. This is so far from the truth that one has to wonder if any of these expert opinions have been formed actually by examining the sites and the corresponding "movement" that are receiving such condemnation. Comments such as the above remind one in an eerie way of the fear-laden panicked criticism of the early gay pride movement; political conservatives and religious fundamentalists condemned that movement on the grounds that it was dangerous—gays were allegedly trying to recruit others into their "life-style."

There are numerous compelling reasons for thinking that this harsh criticism of the pro-ana/mia movement is misguided and over-stated. In the first place, we might point out that there is simply no research data which support any of the claims that these pro-ED expressions make our disordered eating more unhealthy. One would expect that such unanimity of opinion among the "experts" would have at least some basis in research, but it does not. The fear over the pro-ana/mia movement is based largely on the assumption that since disordered eating emerges from a certain psychological perspective, that psychological perspective itself must be as bad as the behavior. Moreover, if one speaks positively about one's disordered eating, one may inadvertently encourage others who are contemplating such behavior (or are "young and impressionable") to begin a life of misery and illness. As Anorexia Truth asserts (above), people who do this must certainly be "sick of mind." While such assumptions may be appealing to the majority of normal eaters, they are still in fact assumptions. Expert opinion needs a more responsible basis.

"Experts" will no doubt point to the fact that pro-ana/mia web-sites often have messages posted from people who say that they want to become anorexic or bulimic, and would like some advice. Insofar as they get advice, so the expert opinion goes, they are being "recruited." Experts should know better than to make such misleading claims. Only an eating disordered person asks for advice on how to become anorexic or bulimic, normal eaters do not request such advice. These sorts of queries do not occur to normal eaters, that's why we call them "normal." If only eating disordered people make such requests to begin with, then responding to them with any kind of advice doesn't count as "recruiting"—the advice seeker was already one of us.

"But you're encouraging people to behave in unhealthy ways!" No, people who request information about how to be anorexic or bulimic and want to behave accordingly are going to act in unhealthy ways whether they receive a response or not. One has to wonder if such expert critics believe also that alcoholics will drink more if they learn what others are drinking, or if smokers will smoke more upon learning their neighbor's favorite brand of cigarettes? It is at least suspiciously inconsistent for doctors and therapists and members of university "eating disorder treatment teams" to repeatedly tell us that *isolation* exacerbates our condition and then insist that we refrain from reaching out to others who are similarly affected. It is exponentially more suspicious when such dictates are made without the aid of any confirming research data.

Secondly, every such site (which is still permitted to exist), without exception has warnings posted which acknowledge that there is open discussion of eating disorders that may be difficult for some people to handle. They tell the reader, prior to entering the site, that disordered eating is not fun and not healthy and that one who eats normally should not seek to do otherwise. The point of noting this fact is that based on the content of these sites there seems to be no grounds for thinking that they are being dishonest or sneaky about "promoting a life-style" or "recruiting" anyone.

Thirdly, once one begins reading what is posted on some of these web-sites, one learns very quickly that a significant portion of the "information" offered is nothing more than advertisements for diet pills and other prescriptions believed to help with weight loss. This information appears to be presented by people who are looking for places to post free online advertisements. This finding is interesting indeed, especially in light of the fact (as we pointed out in chapter 2) that pharmaceutical companies have had very little success in formulating prescription drugs that are effective in the treatment of disordered eating. They appear to be making up for this failure with the sale of weight loss products, and *they* are certainly in no hurry to shut down the pro-ana/mia web-sites! Other kinds of meaningless posts on these web-sites include pleas for people to stop reading such material and get help (submitted no doubt by well-meaning normal eaters and "experts"), links to pornography sites, and other irrelevancies.

Fourth, among the information posted by people with disordered eating, some has to do with sharing information about what one can do to prevent specific health problems that can result from disordered eating. One might, for example, find discussions about which vitamins or other substances are depleted in the body by specific behaviors such as starving, over-exercising, excessive laxative use, or vomiting. People often tell each other what remedies or supplements worked for them in preserving a modicum of health during their time of disordered eating. One such web-site which I visited many years ago contained an interesting dialogue concerning brushing of teeth by bulimics. Someone had suggested that immediately after vomiting one should not brush one's teeth but rather should rinse one's mouth with water and baking soda (or some similar solution). The reason given for this suggestion was that vomiting soaks the teeth in stomach acid which softens tooth enamel. Brushing right away can result in excessive loss of tooth enamel, since one is brushing when the enamel is most soft and vulnerable. If the stomach acid were neutralized first by way of the soda rinse, much of the enamel could be preserved.

The person who suggested this came under significant criticism from one of the well-meaning normal eaters on the site, allegedly for "encouraging" and "promoting" unhealthy behavior. It was clear, however, that the rinsing recommendation was not encouraging anything except preservation of teeth. That was in 1995. Today, most dentists still will not make this suggestion to their bulimic patients because they believe that it "encourages" us. It is strange indeed that so many people in the healthcare field are able to recognize that recommending the use of condoms does not encourage a life-style of sexual promiscuity, and that recommending that drug addicts use clean needles does not promote a life-style of addiction. Why they would think differently about this particular scenario is difficult to figure out. At any rate, I personally took the advice of the person who suggested the soda rinse, and although I spent years vomiting many times each day, I never received cavities or lost tooth enamel in so doing. I cannot imagine that I would be better off today having not gotten that advice and, as a result, lost most of my teeth. Whoever posted that advice, if you happen to read this book, thank you!

Finally, as many newspaper reporters and eating disorders authorities have pointed out, there are those people on the pro-ana/mia sites who celebrate and embrace their disordered eating and express only the desire to maintain their unhealthy behaviors. They ask others for advice on how to starve or purge more efficiently, and others give them advice. Although the media's portrayal of these sites is largely over-stated, the trading of tips and tricks does in fact happen on these web-sites—some people really do promote actively disordered eating.

So what? The idea that we would be better off if we didn't say such things about our disordered eating is—again—not founded on any data. For many of us, the alternative to these pro-ana/mia chat boards is silence—we just don't have anyone else to talk to about this stuff. I was in precisely this situation in the early to mid 1990s, and at that time there were no such pro-ana web-sites (neither were there yet any pro-recovery web-sites). I was fortunate to find a chat board for people with obsessive compulsive disorder, and there were several other regulars there who were bulimic and anorexic. I was of the opinion that "rule number one" regarding my disordered eating was that no one would ever find out about it. This rule was not a product of any fear of embarrassment, but was rather intended to enable me to maintain my actions. I knew full well that once people knew what I was doing, I would be hounded into getting help of some kind—and I didn't want help, I loved my disordered eating.

As might be expected, "rule number one" resulted in a great loneliness—my disordered eating, although severe and protracted, remained undisclosed and hidden from everyone for many years. The OCD chat board became an avenue for communication that was vitally important to me. I was able to tell people what I thought and how I felt about my disordered eating, get some feedback, and remain completely anonymous. It would be difficult indeed to overstate the relief that this outlet provided.

In his outstanding psychological account of inward torment entitled *The Sickness Unto Death*, 19th century Danish philosopher Søren Kierkegaard noted the life-saving potential of being able to share one's secret suffering (one's "introversion") with even just one other person:

> If this introversion is absolutely maintained, *omnibus numeris absoluta*, then suicide will be the danger nearest to him. The common run of men have of course no presentiment of what such an introvert is capable of bearing; if they were to come to know it, they would be astonished. If on the other hand he talks to someone, if to one single man he opens his heart, he is in all probability strained to so high a tension, or so much let down, that suicide does not result from introversion. Such an introvert, with one person privy to his thought, is a whole tone milder than the absolute case. He probably will shun suicide.[18]

It is not so much the *content* of these forums that tells us whether they are good or bad, helpful or harmful—it is their *form*. I could have written anything at all about my experiences on those early OCD sites, and the effect would have been the same. The helpful quality of that experience was derived from the fact that I was beginning to connect with other people. We mentioned in the last two chapters the importance of coming out, connecting with others, and de-isolating. These tasks have to begin somewhere, and it is very often the case that online communities are a less threatening or intimidating starting point than face to face discourse.

Regardless of how disordered one's eating might be, expressing to others in this way that one's behavior is good and desirable is in fact a beginning in assessing one's behavior. It is better to begin assessing one's behavior with at least some positive judgments than with an *a priori* negative point of view, and the fact is that most of us really do—at some point or other—enjoy our disordered eating. These venues, therefore, afford us an important opportunity to be honest about our disordered eating—expressing affection for it if that is how we truly feel. Moreover, since eating disorders (as well as many other "mental illnesses") are widely recognized as being correlated with a significantly increased risk of suicide, and since this risk can be reduced by even minimal contact with others, pro-ana/mia web-sites can potentially be very helpful in this regard.

Any speech, even that which is pro-anorexia or pro-bulimia, is better than silence. The reality of the situation for many of us is that the only real alternative to "pro" discourse is to remain silent. Silence, extreme isolation, never connecting with another person who is eating disordered, these are the principal aggravators of disordered eating and its notable correlation to suicide. No one dies from disordered eating because they speak about it too openly or because they express to others that they don't feel ready to begin a recovery. We should be permitted to speak to each other about our disordered eating, even to promote it openly if we so choose. Shutting down venues in which "pro" discussions are happening sends a very bad message indeed; it says that until we are ready to speak of our disordered eating in a way which explicitly acknowledges it as a disease, we should shut up.

Those who would censor our discussions until such time as we consent to label ourselves as "ill" should find a better way to promote our health. Where are these experts and critics when Barbie dolls are pervasively advertised to our young girls? Barbie has a ball-joint for a stomach and virtual toothpicks for limbs, but Mattel (the manufacturer of Barbie) views the product as some sort of icon for American women. Recently, Mattel introduced a line of Barbie designer clothing for adult women. In an interview about the new line of clothing, Richard Dickson, senior vice president of global consumer marketing and entertainment for Mattel Brands had this to say: "Barbie has a special relationship with women, it takes them back to being a little girl and fantasizing about what they're going to be in the future."[19] Does this count as recruiting people into an "unhealthy life-style?" Where are the critics when the fashion industry teaches women that deathly thin is beautiful?

Where are the critics when we need to be counted and researched? Where was all this concern for things that adversely affect the eating disordered when research established that non-voluntary inpatient treatment makes us twice as likely to die from anorexia?[20] Where were the members of "eating disorder treatment teams" when gastric bypass surgery was shown to precipitate anorexia and bulimia?[21] Does promoting gastric bypass surgery, in light of this documented relationship to facilitating other forms of disordered eating, count as promoting an "unhealthy life-style?" Why, in light of all these other easily identifiable and well documented promoters of disordered eating, is it we sufferers who are criticized merely for speaking out loud? The answer is this: when we talk, the authorities and experts within eating disorders orthodoxy are forced to give an account of their astounding lack of action. Better for them that we keep silent, but not better for us!

These comments are not intended to endorse any particular pro-ana/mia forum or set of ideas, but rather to point out that we already have the beginning of an ED pride movement happening. It is being met with resistance, it is being taken offline, and it is feared by naïve and ignorant researchers, reporters, academics, and the general public. This reaction only serves to demonstrate that we are moving in precisely the right direction.

ED pride is portrayed in the media as "sick of mind," and we are subjected to all manner of attempts at rational persuasion in order that we might come to believe that—above and beyond our actual behaviors—our way of thinking is demented and unhealthy. We need to respond to these tactics in the same way that Socrates responded to Meletus in Plato's *Apology*. Meletus had brought legal charges against Socrates, alleging that Socrates was corrupting the youth of Athens. Socrates pointed out to Meletus that bringing such a charge more than suggested that he, Meletus, had a genuine concern for the youth. When asked to articulate his concern, however, Meletus was silent and unable to respond. His silence was evidence that he obviously had no interest in or special knowledge of the condition of the youth, for had he possessed such knowledge and interest he surely would have articulated it in some fashion. Meletus is refered to as "shameful" by Socrates because Meletus is dishonest and misrepresents himself; he is critical of an alleged trait in others while at the same time openly exhibiting that same trait himself. Similarly, you experts and reporters say you have found what corrupts those of us who are eating disordered; namely, our own open discourse. Tell us then what it is that improves us? You obviously know in view of your keen interest, why not speak up and tell us who or what it is that makes us better? We see that you have long been silent on this matter as there is no medically accepted standard form of treatment for disordered eating. Is this not shameful?

We need to get creative with our ED Pride, and we need to be visible and out. We need to be engaged in some *direct action* which draws attention to our presence, distinguishes our disorder from our disease, and makes it clear that we have been deliberately ignored and are not going to stand for it any longer. Based on what we are able to identify as cultural triggers and reinforcements of disordered eating, we can construct some effective events if enough of us participate. Some of these events might be quiet and thoughtful, and some might be grotesquely sensationalistic—we should do whatever it takes.

We should, for example, target producers of food items who use thin people to advertise foods widely known to be non-nutritive and fattening. Recently, Quaker Oats and Disney combined for just such a venture. "Captain Crunch" cereal was put into boxes on which the Disney character "Kim Possible" was displayed. Kim is a young cartoon female whose waist is only a third as big around as her head, and her waist is always highlighted by a shirt which exposes her midriff. What sort of message is sent to young girls by marketing strategies which place figures of exaggerated thinness on boxes of food made principally of sugar and starch? Is it not a matter of self defense, if even on our daughters' behalf, that we demonstrate against this kind of obvious abuse? Perhaps not all our daughters will be negatively affected by this, but some certainly will be. We need to fight back.

We should target as well certain restaurants that exploit binge eaters by offering low quality food in the form of an all-you-can-eat buffet while advertising themselves as family-oriented, celebratory, or otherwise emotionally happy and comfortable. Such messages obviously promote an environment of excessive over-consuming by targeting people who cope with emotions by eating. When one visits such establishments one finds that the average patron appears anything but happy; many are severely overweight, they are often by themselves, and they rarely smile. One of these feeding troughs could be given precisely what it deserved if, for example, it became completely occupied one day by anorexic women. What would it look like if such an establishment became filled with people who paid the price of admission to the trough, but didn't eat anything, just took up space for several hours? How much money would such a restaurant lose if no tables were vacated for other bewildered and on-looking customers who were anxious to enter and receive their share of happiness? Such an event would get people asking questions and thereby raise some awareness of our existence.

What about the same stunt, but the restaurant is filled with bulimics? Eventually, one can imagine, management might simply have these gorging vomiting customers forcibly removed. Under such circumstances, could we pursue legal action on the grounds of discrimination against a recognized diagnosable disability? Would the Americans with Disabilities Act protect us in such a case? It would be worth finding out. If the ADA could be tested and shown to protect such behavior as not eating in a restaurant but just taking up table space, or repeatedly bingeing and purging (peacefully, in the restroom facilities) in an all-you-can-eat restaurant, disordered eating would skyrocket in the public awareness and receive research funds—even if only from the restaurant lobby.

According to the federal government's understanding of the Americans with Disabilities Act, this scenario is not at all far-fetched. Consider these excerpts from a "Question and Answer" pamphlet currently available from the U.S. Department of Justice, Civil Rights Division:

Q. Are alcoholics covered by the ADA?

A. Yes . . . a person who currently uses alcohol is not automatically denied protection. An alcoholic is a person with a disability and is protected by the ADA if s/he is qualified to perform the essential functions of the job. An employer may be required to provide an accommodation to an alcoholic.[22]

Insofar as physicians and therapists often assert that the mechanics of disordered eating resemble the addictive patterns of alcoholism, it is not too much of a stretch at all to suppose that disordered eating might be considered a disability under the ADA. It should also be noted that alcoholism is not the only condition considered a disability which is also recognized as an "illness." HIV/AIDS has also received protection under the ADA when such has been the basis for discrimination.

Restaurants are also explicitly covered under the ADA as they are considered "public accommodations." The accepted interpretation of the ADA is explicit regarding practices in public accommodations which would limit their services or "screen out" prospective people from being so accommodated:

Q. What are public accommodations?

A. A public accommodation is a private entity that owns, operates, leases, or leases to, a place of public accommodation. Places of public accommodation include a wide range of entities, such as restaurants, hotels, theaters, doctors' offices, pharmacies, retail stores, museums, libraries, parks, private schools, and day care centers.

Q. Will the ADA have any effect on the eligibility criteria used by public accommodations to determine who may receive services?

A. Yes. If a criterion screens out or tends to screen out individuals with disabilities, it may only be used if necessary for the provision of the services. For instance, it would be a violation for a retail store to have a rule excluding all deaf persons from entering the premises, or for a movie theater to exclude all individuals with cerebral palsy. More subtle forms of discrimination are also prohibited. For example, requiring presentation of a driver's license as the sole acceptable means of identification for purposes of paying by check could constitute discrimination against individuals with vision impairments.[23]

Our suggested restaurant scenario in which a few (or a multitude of) anorexics or bulimics pay the stated cost to eat at a buffet, and then either eat nothing at all, or eat—use the restroom in a non-disruptive fashion to purge—and return to the buffet (either of which could easily last for several hours) appears to be within the general parameters of ADA protection. Of course, the point for doing such a thing would be to raise public awareness and challenge public opinion regarding disordered eating. Such an action could reasonably be expected to provoke restaurant management to the point of having participants removed from the premises, and this is exactly what we would be after. Winning an actual settlement would be secondary to the awareness raised by such action. Insofar as there are about 27 million of us at present, we could conceivably occupy a great many of these facilities in all parts of the country on a prearranged day.[24]

Other institutions and corporations that actually promote disordered eating could be similarly targeted, although perhaps in ways that may or may not be quite so protected by law. Animal rights activists, for example, throw blood on people who display fur at a fashion show—how about we throw vomit on fashion moguls who display their clothing on deathly thin models?[25] How about we take a dump truck of vomit to the NIMH or the CDC or the USDA and release it all on their front steps? These examples of direct action will no doubt seem grotesque and awful to those who have not given serious consideration to the oppression of eating disordered people. Why, they might ask, would anyone consider doing such things?

Direct action is a tactic used when pleas for help remain ignored for a very long time. We've already shown that disordered eating affects more people in the United States than any other known medical condition, is the tenth leading cause of death, and yet is minimally researched. What else would it take to point out that our culture has remained deliberately ignorant of eating disorders for as long as it possible could? The pressing question is not so much "why would people do such gruesome things to bring attention to their condition," but rather "why have we not yet stood up or ourselves in this way?"

On a milder note, it would really go a long way to have the simplest of shirts, bumper stickers, hats, bracelets and tattoos that say "ED Pride!" or "Anorexic and Proud!" We can't hide our disordered eating forever. Even if no one finds out about it our lives will be shortened by it. And once we reach a point where we aren't physically ill from our disordered eating, we will want to help our sisters and brothers who still suffer. We are all worth the effort, and we have little to lose.

Direct action is both a vehicle for bringing about change and an expression of Pride. Peaceful direct action is better than any which involves violence, and it is this author's position that only non-violent direct action should ever be used as a tool for change. Having said that, we might well be asked specifically what changes we seek to bring about.

NOTES

1. See especially T. Habermas, "On Uses of History in Psychiatry: Diagnostic Implications for Anorexia Nervosa," *International Journal of Eating Disorders* 38, no. 2 (2005): 167–82. This article traverses an enormous quantity of historical material as well as more recent commentary. Habermas seems particularly interested in retaining weight phobia among the diagnostic criteria, claiming that the arguments for eliminating this diagnostic feature fail on several counts. Our purposes here do not turn on the success or failure of Habermas' position.

The obvious questions associated with this issue are (a) whether anorexia and bulimia as we know them today are continuous with the more ancient accounts of disordered eating, and (b) what might be gained or lost by changing the diagnostic criteria for either or both of these disorders. Concerning (a), Habermas' argument seems to be that the disorders are not continuous because medieval anorexics were religiously motivated whereas their contemporaries have secular/psychological motivations. This is, of course, unconvincing insofar as a person's motives are self-described and must be articulated within the context of one's cultural and conceptual framework. The same motives that would have been articulated in religious terms in the medieval period might not be expressed with the same sort of discourse today since many people do not experience the same religious influences in daily life. Kierkegaard's well known work from 1849, *The Sickness Unto Death* (to which we will refer more explicitly later), shows in dramatic fashion how one and the same "inward" condition might receive either a religious or a psychological articulation, spoken of as "sin" with regard to the former, and as "sickness" with respect to the latter. So, there appears to be no necessity to suppose discontinuity of disorders just because the motives differ in their discursive model of self-report. It is at least curious that Kierkegaard's analysis is historically coincidental with the apparent shift in anorexic motives from the religious to the psychological.

More importantly (for our purposes), with respect to what might be gained or lost by changing the diagnostic criteria for either or both of these disorders, is that none of the motives mentioned in the DSM-IV constitutes a necessary or sufficient condition for diagnosis. As explained in the main text above, the presence of psychological motives in the diagnostic criteria is only useful when indexed to specific observable behaviors.

2. John Stuart Mill, *Utilitarianism* (Indianapolis, Hackett Publishing: 2001). Originally published in 1868. This particular passage is from chapter two.

3. Mill, *Utilitarianism*.

4. University of Pittsburg Department of Psychiatry, "Brave New World: The Role of Genetics in Prevention and Treatment of Eating Disorders," *A Collaborative Study of the Genetics of Anorexia Nervosa and Bulimia Nervosa,* <http://www.wpic.pitt.edu/research/pfanbn/genetics.html>

5. University of Pittsburg Department of Psychiatry, "Brave New World."

6. Centers for Disease Control and Prevention, "Efforts to Reduce or Prevent Obesity," available online: <http://www.cdc.gov/od/oc/media/pressrel/fs050419.htm>. These are not the precise numbers given in the study itself—they have been rounded to the nearest thousand in the CDC's presentation. The precise numbers from the original study are as follows: 33,746 excess deaths for BMI below 18.5; no excess deaths for BMI 18.5–24.9; −86,094 excess deaths for BMI 25–29.9; 29,483 excess deaths for BMI 30–35; and 82,066 excess deaths for BMI over 35. K.M. Flegal, B.I. Graubard, D.F. Williamson, and M.H. Gail, "Excess Deaths Associated with Underweight, Overweight and Obesity," *Journal of the American Medical Association* 293 (2005): 1861–7.

7. BMI is measured according to the following formula: weight in kilograms divided by the square of height in meters. The federal guidelines for weight (BMI) categories cited by Flegal, Graubard, Williamson, and Gail, "Excess Deaths," are: National Institutes of Health, "Panel on the Identification, Evaluation and Treatment of Overweight and Obesity in Adults—The Evidence Report," *Obesity Research* 6 (1998): 51S-209S. Available online from the National Heart, Lung, and Blood Institute: <http://www.nhlbi.nih.gov/guidelines/obesity/ob_home.htm>

8. These "excess deaths" reflect the precise data from Flegal, Graubard, Williamson, and Gail, "Excess Deaths," rather than the CDC's rounded figures.

9. Flegal, Graubard, Williamson, and Gail, "Excess Deaths."

10. NIH, "Panel on the Identification, Evaluation and Treatment of Overweight and Obesity in Adults—The Evidence Report."

11. Flegal, Graubard, Williamson, and Gail, "Excess Deaths."

12. According to the CDC's searchable database for the leading causes of death, in 2002 the top three causes of death were as follows: heart disease killed 696,947 people, malignant neoplasms killed 557,271 people, and 162,672 deaths were attributed to cerebro-vascular causes. <http://webapp.cdc.gov/sasweb/ncipc/leadcaus10.html>

13. See appendices for the DSM-IV diagnostic criteria for anorexia nervosa.

14. *Guiness World Records 2004* (London: Guiness World Records Limited, 2003).

15. Randy Schellenberg, "Sick Minds or Just Human Nature?" *Anorexia Truth*, <http://www.anorexiatruth.com/display.php?page=Pro-Anorexia%20Web%20Sites>

16. Gwen Morrison, "Fatal Trend, Pro-Anorexia Web-sites," *Preteenagers Today,* <http://preteenagerstoday.com/resources/articles/fataltrend.htm>

17. January W. Payne, "No, That's Sick: Pro-Anorexia Web Site Authors Claim The Condition is a 'Lifestyle Choice,'" *Washington Post,* 14 September 2004, HE01.

18. Søren Kierkegaard, *The Sickness Unto Death*, translated by Walter Lowrie. From *A Kierkegaard Anthology*, Edited by Robert Bretall. (Princeton, N.J.: Princeton University Press, 1946). Originally published in Danish in 1849.

19. Angela Moore, "Mattel Launches Barbie Clothes for Women," *Reuters News Service*, New York. 14 October 2005.

20. R. Ramsay, A. Ward, J. Treasure, and G.F. Russell, "Compulsory Treatment in Anorexia Nervosa. Short-Term Benefits and Long-Term Mortality," *British Journal of Psychiatry* 175 (1999): 147–53.

21. J.A. Guisado, F.J. Vaz, J.J. Lopez-Ibor, M.I. Lopez-Ibor, J. del Rio, and M.A. Rubio, "Gastric Surgery and Restraint from Food as Triggering Factors of Eating Disorders in Morbid Obesity," *International Journal of Eating Disorders* 31 (2002): 97–100.

22. United States Equal Employment Opportunity Commission (United States Department of Justice, Civil Rights Division), "Americans with Disabilities Act: Questions and Answers," available online: <http://www.usdoj.gov/crt/ada/q%26aeng02.htm>

23. U.S. Equal Employment Opportunity Commission, "Americans with Disabilities Act."

24. It would also be wise, of course, to consider who the participants might be in a scenario like this. People in recovery might want to let those who are still active in their disordered eating actually do the purging, although others could pretend to do so out of solidarity . . . Perhaps there will be people whose recovery is not so fragile as to be able to handle an event like this, followed by a quick return to healthy eating. Whatever the circumstances, participation would have to be based on a personal decision that one would hope is informed by a responsible understanding of one's medical and psychological condition.

25. Fashion contributors to Mattel's Barbie clothing for adult women include the following: Anna Sui, Anya Hindmarch, Citizens of Humanity, Judith Leiber, Nickel, Not Rational, Paper Denim & Cloth, Stila and Tarina Tarantino.

Chapter Six

Our Demands

We have come to a point in this investigation where we have begun to make positive suggestions concerning appropriate responses to epidemic disordered eating in the United States. In the wake of such critical analyses of current health care practices and the culture by which they are sanctioned, readers who are in fields where they are expected to treat people with disordered eating might well be expected to ask: "Well, what do you want us to do?"

The details that we have been discussing do in fact provide a sufficient basis for several important and constructive conclusions in this regard. These conclusions, however, need to be stated more strongly than a simple expression of "what we want"—and it is certainly within the tradition of a manifesto to have a *list of demands*. To be sure, the inclusion of these demands does not entail any belief in our own ability to guarantee their satisfaction, but we do claim the authority to make these demands.

How is this authority legitimately claimed by us? On the same grounds that any oppressed group has the authority to lay claim to its own freedom. With respect to our disordered eating, we have been held hostage too long. Those who have been granted the responsibility of liberating us have failed us on all fronts; spending virtually no money for research, educating almost no one, providing no standard model for treatment, having no meaningful idea of how many of us exist, and directing criticisms only at those of us who have suffered—either for making bad choices or for speaking too openly—rather than at the multitude of easily identifiable factors that contribute to the prevalence of disordered eating. We claim the authority to make these demands by virtue of the fact that the NIMH has, in its dereliction of duty, abdicated all legitimate claims to authority and trustworthiness.

These demands are simple, reasonable, and practical. These demands are oriented towards freedom from disordered eating for all persons. These demands are not exhaustive, they may be added to as future insights are generated. These demands are drawn strictly from the observations we have made so far, and they are wholly consistent with the manner in which all other major health conditions are already being responded to in the United States.

FIRST DEMAND

Whereas the required prevalence estimates and corresponding research concerning our health and well-being require an ability concretely to distinguish between persons with disordered eating (as well as the manner in which they are afflicted) and those who are not so afflicted, and whereas the present diagnostic criteria are vague and ambiguous in this regard, and whereas this vagueness and ambiguity serve to exclude many eating disordered persons from our community and, hence, from adequate treatment, *we demand that the DSM-IV criteria for the diagnoses of eating disorders be revised.* While numerous detailed revisions may be in order, the primary changes that need to be made are as follows:

- All diagnostic criteria pertaining to weight need to be revised in order more accurately to reflect a responsible account of what constitutes a body weight that is "optimal." According to the findings of Flegal, Graubard, Williamson, and Gail (2005), the BMI indexes in table 6.1 should be used to determine categories of weight.

  These classifications are based on the understanding that what is "optimal" is preferable because it is most conducive to good health. Since Flegal, Graubard, Williamson, and Gail (2005) have demonstrated that a BMI in the 25.0–29.9 range is associated with the fewest excess deaths, this is the optimal range. "Normal" suggests that something is preferable for other reasons, such as social custom and convention, and is therefore not a useful label in this context. Moreover, we have abandoned use of the term "obese" in this classification as it is ambiguous. Insofar as obesity is man-

Table 6.1.   Weight (BMI) Categories, Revised

BMI	Weight Status
Below 18.5	Severely Underweight
18.5–24.9	Underweight
25.0–29.9	Optimal
30.0–34.9	Overweight
35 and above	Severely Overweigh

ifest in varying degrees of severity, "obese" by itself does not specify the degree to which a person's weight (or BMI) deviates from what is optimal.

- We will also be omitting specific psychological criteria from the diagnostic process. The reason for this is that all such diagnostic criteria have no meaning in the absence of identifiable patterns of behavior. Psychological criteria provide neither the necessary nor the sufficient means for diagnosis, and they change over time as the social discourse for articulating one's motives changes. It may well be the case that disordered eating is "goal oriented" whereas unhealthy eating that is attributable to other medical causes is not. If the complete omission of psychological criteria is found in practice to be less useful, then the criteria below could certainly be amended to include reference to motive by way of the unspecified notion of "goal oriented behavior."
- EDNOS (Eating Disorder—Not Otherwise Specified) should be eliminated from the list of diagnoses, as it constitutes an unhelpful ambiguity and serves to marginalize the illnesses of the many people who currently fall within this category. Treatment providers who work in the field of eating disorders are aware that the EDNOS diagnosis is designed to accommodate persons suffering from conditions commonly referred to as binge eating disorder, sub-threshold anorexia, and sub-threshold bulimia; these conditions should, therefore, be more specifically accommodated in the diagnostic process.
- As a diagnosable eating disorder, binge eating disorder needs to be listed as recognizable according these specific criteria:

  1. Recurrent episodes of binge eating. An episode of binge eating is characterized by eating, in a discrete period of time (e.g., within any 2-hour period), an amount of food that is definitely larger than most people would eat during a similar period of time and under similar circumstances.
  2. Overweight or severely overweight, according to the revised weight (BMI) categories in table 6.1.

Since the CDC and NIMH have already stated in their literature that binge eaters suffer disproportionately from being overweight or severely overweight, the diagnostic criteria for binge eating disorder need to include being overweight or severely overweight at least as probable indicators and common symptoms of this condition. These criteria not only have the advantage of making binge eating disorder diagnosable in a concrete way, but they also provide for an ability to diagnose the disorder in gradations according to severity. "Grade 1 binge eating disorder," for example, would be the least severe, with the first criterion (recurrent episodes of binge eating) being met, but not the second (overweight). A diagnosis of "grade 2 binge eating disorder" would indicate recurrent episodes of binge eating accompanied by being overweight. The most severe diagnosis, "grade 3 binge eating disorder," would suggest all the criteria for diagnosing "grade 2" and being severely overweight, or having suffered for an extended duration, or having acquired other serious health problems as a direct result of the disorder.

- The current criteria for diagnosing anorexia and bulimia already contain the means by which these conditions may be graded according to severity. Rather than classifying these conditions by severity, however, the present criteria provide different names (or "types"), making use also of the ED-NOS default category. This, again, is unhelpful as it suggests an overly complicated yet ambiguous system. At present, anyone having all the symptoms of anorexia, for example, except one (and it doesn't matter which one) would be classified as EDNOS. It would be clearer to distinguish the diagnostic criteria for anorexia from other symptoms that are indicators of severity, and classify sufferers according to how many of these latter criteria are manifest. Accordingly, the criteria for anorexia should include the following (with all references to weight informed by table 6.1):

  1. Refusal to maintain body weight at or above a minimally optimal weight for age and height.
  2. Weight loss leading to maintenance of body weight less than 85% of what is minimally optimal for age and height.
  3. Failure to make expected weight gain during period of growth, leading to body weight less than 85% of what is minimally optimal for age and height.

By this standard, manifesting any one of these conditions would constitute a diagnosis of "grade 1 anorexia nervosa." Other symptoms usually considered diagnostic are in fact more appropriately understood as indicators of severity. Severity could, for example, be indicated by such symptoms as being significantly below 85% of minimally optimal weight, or amenorrhea, or having suffered for an extended period of time, or having acquired other physical symptoms of deteriorating health such as decreased bone density, etc. "Grade two anorexia nervosa" would be diagnosed therefore based on manifesting any one of the initial conditions above in conjunction with any one of these indicators of severity. The diagnosis of "grade 3 anorexia nervosa" could be made based on manifesting any one of the initial conditions above in conjunction with any two or more indicators of severity.

- Similar to the gradations of binge eating disorder and anorexia, bulimia could easily be diagnosed on such a model. The criteria for diagnosing bulimia should include:

1. Recurrent episodes of binge eating. An episode of binge eating is characterized by eating, in a discrete period of time (e.g., within any 2-hour period), an amount of food that is definitely larger than most people would eat during a similar period of time and under similar circumstances.
2. Recurrent inappropriate compensatory behavior in order to prevent weight gain, such as self-induced vomiting, misuse of laxatives, diuretics, enemas, or other medications; fasting, or excessive exercise.

It will be noted that we have omitted the requirement that these symptoms or behaviors be present for three months (twice per week). As with the criteria for anorexia, the duration of the condition is not relevant to establishing whether or not one has it, but is only relevant in regard to severity. "Grade 1 bulimia nervosa" would be diagnosed if both of these criteria are met, for it is only under the conditions that both of these criteria apply that we could distinguish binge eating disorder from bulimia nervosa. "Grade 2 bulimia nervosa" could be used to indicate duration and would be applied in cases when the above criteria had been present for three months (twice per week). "Grade 3 bulimia nervosa" would be used in cases that are exceptionally severe due to the emergence of other health problems, or extreme frequency of bingeing and purging, etc.

This basic diagnostic model is already apparent in connection with all other major diseases. How satisfactory or practical would it seem, for example, to receive a diagnosis of "cancer NOS," or "cardiovascular disease NOS," or "diabetes NOS?" Disordered eating is at least as prevalent and often more deadly than these other diseases. It is clearly time, therefore, for a standard diagnostic model.

SECOND DEMAND

Since we know that we outnumber the current sufferers of any other diagnosable condition, and since most medical conditions known to afflict a significant portion of humanity have a designated office at the National Institutes of Health, *we demand the creation of a central organizing body as a member institution of the NIH*. This *National Eating Disorders Institute*

(NEDI) is to be charged with specific tasks with respect to these conditions. For example, NEDI will be responsible for:

- Assessing and making known to the medical community and to the general public the national prevalence of disordered eating according to the revised DSM-IV criteria above.
- Overseeing the appropriate funding and conducting of eating disorders research. Of course, NIMH administration will not be amenable to losing any of their research funds. Any dissent on their part, however, can be easily tempered with the simple reminder that these funds only constitute 1.5 percent of the NIMH budget anyway. Current research can be continued under the auspices of the newly formed NEDI, so NIMH administrators can rest easily knowing that their advancements in the area of eating disorders research will not be lost.
- Making official recommendations regarding methods of treatment. Clearly, significant research will be required in order to make recommendations about an accepted standard model for the treatment of disordered eating. This is, therefore, to be a defining goal of NEDI rather than something immediately forthcoming. While it might be acknowledged that a variety of treatments are available for the different manifestations of disordered eating, specific recovery statistics could provide a basis for endorsing some of these treatments (either treatments that are already in practice, or treatments that emerge as a result of continuing research) as more or less appropriate than others in certain circumstances.
- Disseminating information and promoting awareness. This, ideally, will be accomplished by way of educational programs in primary and secondary schools, advertising campaigns and press releases. Moreover, all promotions of public relations, awareness, etc. should be strictly informed by research data. Included in the overall task of distributing information gleaned from research, NEDI will oversee the Dietary Guidelines Advisory Committee in regular revisions of the *Dietary Guidelines*. Another defining goal of NEDI is the eventual formation of at least one post-graduate degree program which offers a specialization in eating disorders research and treatment.

Again, while it may appear as though these demands are excessive, they should be weighed against the current practices of medical research and care being provided in connection with other medical conditions. If this is done, one sees clearly that these demands are reasonable and consistent with common practice. At present, the facilities charged with tending to the eating problems of the United States population are fractured and disjointed. The NIMH is responsible for researching eating disorders, the CDC is responsible for tracking their prevalence (at least with regard to "obesity"), and the USDA loosely supervises the construction of the *Dietary Guidelines*. It is not apparent, however, that any of these agencies has significant discourse with the others or knows what they are doing. By analogy, it would be medically irresponsible indeed if someone were to propose the dissolution of the National Cancer Institute and the subsequent handling of all cancer research and treatment recommendations by the "National Institute of Physical Health," selective tracking of prevalence by the CDC alone, and constructing recommendations on how to avoid getting cancer by the Environmental Protection Agency. This, however, is precisely what we have been putting up with in the field of eating disorders for years – it is clearly time for the National Eating Disorders Institute.

THIRD DEMAND

As the CDC currently requires that all major diseases be reported and tracked, and since disordered eating is in fact a major disease (even by current irresponsible NIMH standards), *we demand that healthcare providers be required to report the diagnoses of eating disorders to NEDI and to the CDC* in the same way they are required to do so on behalf of the sufferers of other known illnesses. Failure to report instances of a medical condition that is known to exist in epidemic proportions within the general population constitutes one more way in which sufferers of disordered eating are systematically excluded from the healthcare system. Since our recovery can only be maximally facilitated by our full integration into the healthcare system, our diagnoses need to be treated with the same serious attention nationally as the diagnoses of other serious illnesses.

How long would we be willing to remain idle and watch people losing their lives to a flu epidemic, knowing all the while that one of the reasons for the deaths of our loved ones was that the disease was permitted to spread unchecked with no requirement to report it to any official healthcare agency? If a person is vomiting because of the flu, though it be a mild flu that lasts only a few days, attending physicians would nonetheless be required to report such a case to the CDC. But if a bulimic person is vomiting, though it be a severe case that lasts for years, no such reporting is presently required. This needs to change. Since one of the purposes of the National Eating Disorders Institute will be to track accurately the prevalence of eating disorders, and since this can only be done when the rate at which new cases emerge is known, this reporting clearly constitutes an important element in our ability to free sufferers from these conditions.

FOURTH DEMAND

Since it is common and appropriate practice for specialized healthcare providers to be monitored by a governing body which establishes criteria for licensure in their specialty, and since the treatment of disordered eating reasonably constitutes a medical specialization, *we demand regulated licensure for eating disorders treatment providers, a minimum requirement for which will be successful completion of the core curriculum in an accredited program of study.* One of the principal reasons for the present mindless and unorganized plurality of eating disorders treatment options is that there are literally no legal requirements for charging money in exchange for providing "treatment." Currently, anyone who believes her/himself to have an answer to this epidemic problem can open an office and provide whatever services they want under the guise of "treatment." While we do not deny the effectiveness of some of the "treatments" being offered, we do recognize that many such enterprises are nothing more than attempts to prey upon desperate and unwitting sufferers.

Peddlers of such cancer cures as snake oil, "magic" powders, and colored light bulbs were held in great disrepute 150 years ago. Even though some of their "patients" may in fact have recovered, it was easy to see that they were capitalizing on someone's suffering. Hence, it seemed a good idea to regulate, by way of established practices of licensure, who was permitted to treat this disease. It is clearly time for disordered eating to be treated as seriously. Or is it heinous to exploit the sufferers of one deadly disease, but not others?

FIFTH DEMAND

Some treatments need to be discontinued, even though they are currently practiced by licensed individuals. Specifically, some current practices in the treatment of disordered eating have been demonstrated to be highly dangerous and of questionable efficacy. Therefore, *we demand an immediate moratorium on gastric bypass surgeries and all court ordered (involuntary) treatments of anorexia nervosa.*

• The moratorium on gastric bypass surgery is necessitated by way of the growing concerns within the medical research community about the procedure's overall efficacy and safety. Courcoulas and Flum (2005) have explained why ethical concerns preclude our ability to demonstrate the efficacy of this procedure according to a standard experimental model which employs a control group. Zingmond, McGory, Ko (2005) have offered exhausting evidence that gastric bypass surgery has an enormous impact on health care costs, with patient's being hospitalized twice as much after surgery as before. Guisado, Vaz, Lopez-Ibor, Lopez-Ibor, del Rio, and Rubio (2002) have shown us that this procedure is known to precipitate other forms of disordered eating such as anorexia and bulimia.

• The saving of lives also forms the basis for the moratorium on all involuntary (court ordered) treatment for sufferers of anorexia. We know that such involuntary treatment makes us sicker. Concerns expressed from within the medical research community form the basis for this claim as well. Sullivan (1995) has established a reliable mortality rate for anorexics generally—5.6 percent per decade. Watson, Bowers, and Andersen (2001) have established that there is no significant difference in severity of condition between those entering treatment voluntarily and those entering treatment involuntarily. Ramsay, Ward, Treasure, and Russell (1999) have shown, however, that involuntary patients have more than twice the mortality rate as the general population of anorexics—12.7 percent per decade.

It is certainly true that *without* court orders of this kind, some anorexics will die. It is also true that *with* such court orders, some anorexics will die. The obvious goal is to choose the scenario that involves the fewest deaths. To this end, it should be very clear that taking some of the people from the general group of anorexics and forcing them by court order into a sub-category of anorexics that has a much higher mortality rate than the general anorexic population is absurdly counterproductive. If we know, as the research demonstrates, that this approach *doubles* one's chance of dying, then we know also that such court orders are not justifiable.

In cases involving other diseases, authoritative healthcare agencies shun treatments the efficacy of which remains undemonstrated, and they ban treatments that are proven to make the patient worse. Why, then, in light of this research data would gastric bypass surgeries and involuntary treatments of anorexics still be practiced? It is clearly time to bring the legal and medical aspects of treatment for disordered eating out of medievalism and into the twenty-first century.

SIXTH DEMAND

The information presented in this book is not esoteric, and it is not in any way hidden from full public view. Anyone who wants to find out the "big picture" on eating disorders can easily obtain and decipher all the documents that were consulted in the preparation of this book. But if this information is so readily available, why has it not been taken seriously? *We demand that sanctioned representatives from the NIH, NIMH, CDC, and USDA make a full and public apology to the families of those who have not survived their disordered eating.* The healthcare system from which we have been pervasively excluded has saved money at the expense of our grandparents and parents, our siblings and spouses and friends, our children and grandchildren. It is time to secure amends for their suffering and prevent the similar suffering of others. Such amends and prevention must come by way of the satisfaction of these demands.

That these demands appear extreme is indeed a telling fact about the way we think about disordered eating in medicine and in our culture. Nothing has been demanded here that has not previously existed for sufferers of all other known diseases for decades. So these demands are not extreme, the conditions that have necessitated these demands are extreme. But that is about to change . . .

Appendix A

Diagnostic Criteria for Eating Disorders, DSM-IV

DIAGNOSTIC AND STATISTICAL MANUAL OF MENTAL DISORDERS (4TH ED.). AMERICAN PSYCHIATRIC ASSOCIATION. WASHINGTON, DC. 1994

307.1 Anorexia Nervosa

A. Refusal to maintain body weight at or above a minimally normal weight for age and height (e.g., weight loss leading to maintenance of body weight less than 85% of that expected; or failure to make expected weight gain during period of growth, leading to weight less than 85% of that expected).
B. Intense fear of gaining weight or becoming fat, even though underweight.
C. Disturbance in the way in which one's body weight or shape is experienced, undue influence of body shape on self-evaluation, or denial of the seriousness of the current low body weight.
D. In postmenarcheal females, amenorrhea, i.e., the absence of at least three consecutive menstrual cycles.

307.50 Eating Disorder NOS (Not Otherwise Specified)

The Eating Disorder Not Otherwise Specified category is for disorders of eating that do not meet the criteria for any specific Eating Disorder. Examples include:

1. For females, all of the criteria for Anorexia Nervosa are met except that the individual has regular menses.
2. All of the criteria for Anorexia Nervosa are met except that, despite significant weight loss, the individual's weight is in the normal range.

3. All of the criteria for Bulimia Nervosa are met except that the binge eating and inappropriate compensatory mechanisms occur at a frequency of less than twice a week or for a duration of less than 3 months.
4. The regular use of inappropriate compensatory behavior by an individual of normal body weight after eating small amounts of food (e.g., self-induced vomiting after the consumption of two cookies).
5. Repeatedly chewing and spitting out, but not swallowing, large amounts of food.
6. Binge-eating disorder: recurrent episodes of binge eating in the absence of the regular use of compensatory behaviors characteristic of Bulimia Nervosa (Binge eat, but do not purge).

307.51 Bulimia Nervosa

A. Recurrent episodes of binge eating. An episode of binge eating is characterized by both of the following:
   (1) Eating, in a discrete period of time (e.g., within any 2-hour period), an amount of food that is definitely larger than most people would eat during a similar period of time and under similar circumstances.
   (2) A sense of lack of control over eating during the episode (e.g., a feeling that one cannot stop eating or control what or how much one is eating).
B. Recurrent inappropriate compensatory behavior in order to prevent weight gain, such as self-induced vomiting, misuse of laxatives, diuretics, enemas, or other medications; fasting, or excessive exercise.
C. The binge eating and inappropriate compensatory behaviors occur, on average, at least twice a week for three months.
D. Self-evaluation is unduly influenced by body shape and weight.
E. The disturbance does not occur exclusively during episodes of Anorexia Nervosa.

Diagnostic Criteria for Eating Disorders, ICD-10

INTERNATIONAL STATISTICAL CLASSIFICATION OF DISEASES AND RELATED HEALTH PROBLEMS, 10TH REVISION. WORLD HEALTH ORGANIZATION (2003)

F50.0 Anorexia Nervosa

A disorder characterized by deliberate weight loss, induced and sustained by the patient. It occurs most commonly in adolescent girls and young women, but adolescent boys and young men may also be affected, as may children approaching puberty and older women up to the menopause. The disorder is associated with a specific psychopathology whereby a dread of fatness and flabbiness of body contour persists as an intrusive overvalued idea, and the patients impose a low weight threshold on themselves. There is usually undernutrition of varying severity with secondary endocrine and metabolic changes and disturbances of bodily function. The symptoms include restricted dietary choice, excessive exercise, induced vomiting and purgation, and use of appetite suppressants and diuretics.

F50.1 Atypical Anorexia Nervosa

Disorders that fulfil some of the features of anorexia nervosa but in which the overall clinical picture does not justify that diagnosis. For instance, one of the key symptoms, such as amenorrhoea or marked dread of being fat, may be absent in the presence of marked weight loss and weight-reducing behaviour. This diagnosis should not be made in the presence of known physical disorders associated with weight loss.

F50.2 Bulimia Nervosa

A syndrome characterized by repeated bouts of overeating and an excessive preoccupation with the control of body weight, leading to a pattern of overeating followed by vomiting or use of purgatives. This disorder shares many psychological features with anorexia nervosa, including an overconcern with body shape and weight. Repeated vomiting is likely to give rise to disturbances of body electrolytes and physical complications. There is often, but not always, a history of an earlier episode of anorexia nervosa, the interval ranging from a few months to several years.

F50.3 Atypical Bulimia Nervosa

Disorders that fulfil some of the features of bulimia nervosa, but in which the overall clinical picture does not justify that diagnosis. For instance, there may be recurrent bouts of overeating and overuse of purgatives without significant weight change, or the typical overconcern about body shape and weight may be absent.

F50.4 Overeating Associated with Other Psychological Disturbances

Overeating due to stressful events, such as bereavement, accident, childbirth, etc.

Appendix C

Diagnostic Criteria for Eating Disorders, NHS Primary Care Protocols for Common Mental Illness; Protocol III: Eating Disorders (18+ Years)

PRIMARY CARE PROTOCOLS FOR COMMON MENTAL ILLNESSES. NATION HEALTH SERVICE. CROYDON HEALTH AUTHORITY, 2001

Anorexia Nervosa

- Body weight maintained 15% below that expected for age and height/BMI <17.5kg/m2
- Weigh loss self-induced by
  —restriction of intake
  —self-induced vomiting
  —self-induced purging
  —excessive exercise
  —use of appetite suppressant or diurctics
- Morbid dread of fatness (over-valued idea)
- Self-set low weight threshold
- Disturbance of endocrine function to produce amenorrhoea in women and loss of sexual interest and potency in men (in prepubertal onset there is a delay of puberty and growth restriction

Bulimia Nervosa

- Bingeing, with preoccupation with food and craving of the same
- Attempts to counteract excess calorie intake by
  —self-induced vomiting
  —self-induced purging

—alternating periods of starvation and bingeing

—use of appetite suppressants, diuretics, thyroid preparations or, in diabetes, neglect of insulin treatment

- Morbid dread of fatness
- Self-set low weight threshold
- Possible history of anorexia nervosa or atypical anorexia nervosa

Bibliography

BOOKS

Bogdanovic, S. *Opportunities In Obesity, Anorexia, and Bulimia: A Report for Scrip World Pharmaceutical News* London: PJB Publications Ltd, 1992.

Bretall, Robert ed. *A Kierkegaard Anthology* Princeton, NJ: Princeton University Press, 1946.

Brownell, K., and Fairburn, C. eds. *Eating Disorders and Obesity: A Comprehensive Handbook*. New York: Guilford, 1995.

Cicchetti, D., and Cohen, D. eds. *Developmental Psychopathology—Volume 2: Risk, Disorder, and Adaptation*. New York: Wiley, 1995.

Crowther, M., Tennenbaum, D., Hobfoll, S., and Stephens, M. eds. *The Etiology of Bulimia Nervosa: The individual and Familial Context*. Washington, D.C.: Taylor & Francis, 1992.

Diagnostic and Statistical Manual of Mental Disorders 4th ed. Washington, D.C.: American Psychiatric Association.1994.

Fairburn, C., and Wilson, G. eds. *Binge Eating: Nature, Assessment, and Treatment*. New York: Guilford, 1993.

Gilligan, C. *In a Different Voice: Psychological Theory and Women's Development*. Cambridge: Harvard University Press; Reissue edition, 1993.

Gordon, R. *Anorexia and Bulimia: Anatomy of a Social Epidemic*. New York: Blackwell, 1990.

Guiness World Records 2004. London: Guiness World Records Limited, 2003.

Haye, H. *Radically Gay: Gay Liberation in the Words of Its Founder*, edited by Will Rosco. Boston: Beacon Press, 1997.

Kierkegaard, S. *The Sickness Unto Death*, translated by Alastair Hannay. New York: Penguin Books, 1989.

Mill, John Stuart. *Utilitarianism*, 2nd ed., edited by George Sher. Indianapolis: Hackett Publishing Company, 2001.

Plato. *The Trial and Death of Socrates*, 3rd ed., translated by G.M.A. Grube. Indianapolis: Hackett Publishing Company, 2000.

Primary Care Protocols for Common Mental Illnesses. London: Nation Health Service, 2001.

Robins, L., and Regier, D. eds. *Psychiatric Disorders in America, The Epidemiologic Catchment Area Study*. New York: The Free Press. 1990.

International Statistical Classification of Diseases and Related Health Problems, 10th revision. World Health Organization, 2003.

ARTICLES FROM PROFESSIONAL
JOURNALS AND CONFERENCES

Allaz, A., M. Bernstein, P. Rouget, M. Archinard, and A. Morabia. "Body Weight Preoccupation in Middle-age and Ageing Women: A General Population Survey." *International Journal of Eating Disorders* 23, no. 3 (1998): 287–94.

American Psychiatric Association Work Group on Eating Disorders. "Practice Guideline for the Treatment of Patients with Eating Disorders (revision)." *American Journal of Psychiatry* 157, no. 1 (2000): 1S-39S.

Banasiak S., S. Paxton, and P. Hay. "Evaluating Accessible Treatments for Bulimic Eating Disorders in Primary Care." Research paper University of Melbourne, and University of Adelaide, 1998.

Beck, D., R. Casper, and A. Andersen. "Truly Late Onset of Eating Disorders: A Study of 11 Cases Averaging 60 Years of Age at Presentation." *International Journal of Eating Disorders* 20, no. 4 (1996): 389–95.

Birmingham, L.C, J. Su, J.A. Hlynsky, E.M. Goldner, and M. Gao. "The Mortality Rate from Anorexia Nervosa." *International Journal of Eating Disorders* 38, no. 2 (2005): 143–6.

Bruce, B., and W.S. Agras. "Binge Eating in Females: A Population-Based Investigation." *International Journal of Eating Disorders* 12 (1992): 365–73.

Courcoulas, A.P., and D.R. Flum. "Filling the Gaps in Bariatric Surgical Research." *Journal of the American Medical Association* 294, no. 15 (2005): 1957–60.

Flegal, K.M., B.I. Graubard, D.F. Williamson, and M.H. Gail. "Excess Deaths Associated with Underweight, Overweight and Obesity." *Journal of the American Medical Association* 293 (2005): 1861–7.

Garry, J., S. Morrissey, and L. Whetstone. "Substance Use and Weight Loss Tactics Among Middle School Youth." *International Journal of Eating Disorders* 33, no. 1 (2002): 55–63.

Gleaves, D., G. Post, K. Eberenz, and W. Davis. "A Report of 497 Women Hospitalized   for the Treatment of Bulimia Nervosa." *Eating Disorders: The Journal of Treatment and Prevention* 1 (1993): 134–46.

Guisado, J.A., F.J. Vaz, J.J. Lopez-Ibor, M.I. Lopez-Ibor, J. del Rio, and M.A. Rubio. "Gastric Surgery and Restraint from Food as Triggering Factors of Eating Disorders in Morbid Obesity." *International Journal of Eating Disorders* 31 (2002): 97–100.

Habermas, T. "On Uses of History in Psychiatry: Diagnostic Implications for Anorexia Nervosa." *International Journal of Eating Disorders* 38, no. 2 (2005): 167–82.

Hewitt, P.L., S. Coren, and G.D. Steel. "Death from Anorexia Nervosa: Age Span and Sex Differences." *Aging and Mental Health* 5 (2001): 41–6.

Hsu L. "Epidemiology of Eating Disorders." *Psychiatric Clinics of North America* 19, (1996): 681–700.

Hsu, L. and B. Zimmer. "Eating Disorders in Old Age." *International Journal of Eating Disorders* 7, no. 1 (1988): 133–8.

Kjelsas, E., C. Bjornstrom,and K. Gotestam. "Prevalence of Eating Disorders in Female and Male Adolescents (14–15 years)." *Eating Behaviors* 5, no. 1 (2004): 13–25.

Lewis, D., and F. Cachelin. "Body Image Dissatisfaction and Eating Attitudes in Midlife and Elderly Women." *Eating Disorders: The Journal of Treatment and Prevention* 9, no. 1 (2001): 29–39.

Lowe M., W. Davis, R. Annunziato, and D. Lucks. "Inpatient Treatment for Eating Disorders: Outcome at Discharge and 3-Month Follow-up." *Eating Behaviors* 4 (2003): 385–97.

Lowe, B., S. Zipfel, C. Buchholz, Y. Dupont, D.L. Reas, and W. Herzog. "Long-Term Outcome of Anorexia Nervosa in a Prospective 21-Year Follow-up Study." *Psychological Medicine* 31, (2001): 881–90.

Mermelstein, H.T., and R. Basu. "Can You Ever be Too Old to be Too Thin? Anorexia Nervosa in a 92 Year Old Woman." *International Journal of Eating Disorders* 30, no. 1 (2001): 123–6.

Narrow, W. E. "One-Year Prevalence of Depressive Disorders Among Adults 18 and Over in the U.S.: NIMH ECA Prospective Data. Population Estimates Based on U.S. Census Estimated Residential Population Age 18 and Over on July 1, 1998," Unpublished.

——. "One-Year Prevalence of Mental Disorders, Excluding Substance Use Disorders, in the U.S.: NIMH ECA Prospective Data. Population estimates based on U.S. Census estimated residential population age 18 and over on July 1, 1998," Unpublished.

Nielsen, S., C. Emborg, and A.G. Mølbak. "Mortality in Concurrent Type 1 Diabetes and Anorexia Nervosa." *Diabetes Care* 25, no. 2 (2002).

Ramsay, R., A. Ward, J. Treasure, and G.F. Russell. "Compulsory Treatment in Anorexia Nervosa. Short-Term Benefits and Long-Term Mortality." *British Journal of Psychiatry* 175 (1999): 147–53.

Reas, D.L., E. Kjelsas, T. Heggestad, L. Eriksen, S. Nielsen, F. Gjertsen, and K.G. Gotestam. "Characteristics of Anorexia Nervosa-Related Deaths in Norway (1992–2000): Data from the National Patient Register and the Causes of Death Register." *International Journal of Eating Disorders* 37, no. 3 (2005): 181–7.

Reimann, B.C., R.J. McNally, and A. Meier. "Anorexia Nervosa in an Elderly Man." *International Journal of Eating Disorders* 14, (1993): 501–4.

Santry, H.P., D.L. Gillen, and D.S. Lauderdale. "Trends in Bariatric Surgical Procedures." *Journal of the American Medical Association* 294, no. 15 (2005): 1909–17.

Shisslak, C.M., M. Crago, and L.S. Estes. "The Spectrum of Eating Disturbances." *International Journal of Eating Disorders* 18, no. 3 (1995): 209–19.

Spitzer, R.L., S. Yanovski, T. Wadden, R. Wing, M.D. Marcus, A. Stunkard, M. Devlin, J. Mitchell, D. Hasin, and R.L. Horne. "Binge Eating Disorder: Its Further Validation in a Multisite Study." *International Journal of Eating Disorders* 13, no. 2 (1993): 137–53.

Sullivan P. "Mortality in Anorexia Nervosa." *American Journal of Psychiatry* 152 (1995): 1073–4.

Sullivan P., C. Bulik, J. Fear, and A. Pickering. "Outcome of Anorexia Nervosa: A Case-Control Study." *American Journal of Psychiatry* 155 (1998): 939–46.

Watson, T., W. Bowers, and A. Andersen. "Involuntary Treatment of Patients with Eating Disorders." *Eating Disorders Review* 12, no. 2 (2001).

Webster P., U. Schmidt, and J. Treasure. "'Reforming the Mental Health Act': Implications of the Government's White Paper for the Management of Patients with Eating Disorders." *Psychiatric Bulletin* 27 (2003): 364–6.

Wolfe, B.M., and J.M. Morton. "Weighing in on Bariatric Surgery." *Journal of the American Medical Association* 294, no. 15 (2005): 1960–3.

Zingmond, D.S., M.L. McGory, and C.Y. Ko. "Hospitalization Before and After Gastric Bypass Surgery." *Journal of the American Medical Association* 294, no. 15 (2005): 1918–24.

ONLINE ARTICLES AND GOVERNMENT PUBLICATIONS (ALL ONLINE ARTICLES ACCESSED AS RECENTLY AS JANUARY, 2006)

American Cancer Society. "Cancer Facts & Figures 2004." <http://www.cancer.org/downloads/STT/CAFF_finalPWSecured.pdf>

American Heart Association. "Know the Facts Get the Stats." <http://www.americanheart.org/presenter.jhtml?identifier=3000996>

American Psychiatric Association. "Practice Guideline for the Treatment of Patients with Bipolar Disorder (Revision)." <http://www.psych.org/psych_pract/treatg/pg/bipolar_revisebook_3.cfm>

Centers For Disease Control and Prevention. "Efforts to Reduce or Prevent Obesity." <http://www.cdc.gov/od/oc/media/pressrel/fs050419.htm>

——. "Frequently Asked Questions: Overweight and Obesity." <http://www.cdc.gov/nccdphp/dnpa/obesity/faq.htm#costs>

——. "Overweight and Obesity: Contributing Factors." <http://www.cdc.gov/nccdphp/dnpa/obesity/contributing_factors.htm>

Ellis, C., and C. Schnoes. "Eating Disorder: Pica." *eMedicine*, 2002. <http://www.emedicine.com/ped/topic1798.htm>

Insel, T. "Testimony on Fiscal Year 2005 Hearing on Substance Abuse and Mental Health before the House Subcommittee on Labor-HHS-Education Appropriations." <http://www.nimh.nih.gov/about/2005budget.pdf>

International Diabetes Federation. "Did You Know?" <http://www.idf.org/home/index .cfm?node=37>

Makino, M., K. Tsuboi, and L. Dennerstein. "Prevalence of Eating Disorders: A Comparison Of Western and Non-Western Countries." *Medscape General Medicine* 6, no. 3 (2004). <http://www.medscape.com/viewarticle/487413>

Morrison, G. "Fatal Trend: Pro-Anorexia Web Sites." *Preteenagerstoday.com* <http:// preteenagerstoday.com/resources/articles/fataltrend.htm>

MyPyramid.gov. "Johanns Reveals USDA'S Steps to a Healthier You." Press Release, April 19, 2005. <http://mypyramid.gov/global_nav/media_press_release.html>

Nation Health Service. "Protocol III: Eating Disorders (18+ Years)." in *Primary Care Protocols for Common Mental Illness.* <http://www.rcpsych.ac.uk/college/sig/ pcProtocol.pdf>

National Cancer Institute. "Secondhand Smoke: Questions and Answers." <http:// www.cancer.gov/cancertopics/factsheet/Tobacco/ETS>

National Eating Disorders Association. "Health Consequences of Eating Disorders." <http://www.nationalcatingdisorders.org/p.asp?WebPage_ID=286&Profile_ID=41 143>

National Institute of Mental Health. "Anxiety Disorders." 1994, NIH Publication No. 3879.

———. "Anxiety Disorders Research at the National Institute of Mental Health." 1999, NIH Publication No. 99–4504.

———. "Autism Spectrum Disorders (Pervasive Developmental Disorders)." 2004, NIH Publication No.04-5511. <http://www.nimh.nih.gov/healthinformation/ autismmenu.cfm>

———. "Depression." 2000, NIH Publication No. 00-3561.

———. "Eating Disorders: Facts About Eating Disorders and the Search for Solutions." 2001, NIH Publication No. 01-4901. <http://www.nimh.nih.gov/publicat/ eatingdisorders.cfm#ed1>

———. "Fiscal Year 2005 President's Budget Request." <http://www.nimh.nih.gov/ about/mech005.pdf>

———. "Going to Extremes: Bipolar Disorder." 2001, NIH Publication No. 01-4595.

———. "The Numbers Count: Mental Disorders in America." 2001, NIH Publication No. 01-4584.

———. "When Someone Has Schizophrenia." 2001, NIH Publication No. 01-4599.

National Institute of Neurological Disorders and Stroke. "Brain Basics: Preventing Stroke." <http://www.ninds.nih.gov/disorders/stroke/preventing_stroke.htm>

National Institutes of Health. "Binge Eating Disorder." 2004, NIH Publication No. 04-3589. <http://win.niddk.nih.gov/publications/binge.htm>

———. "Panel on the Identification, Evaluation and Treatment of Overweight and Obesity in Adults—The Evidence Report," *Obesity Research* 6 (1998): 51S-209S. NIH Publication Number 98-4083. Available online from the National Heart, Lung, and Blood Institute: <http://www.nhlbi.nih.gov/guidelines/obesity/ob _home.htm>

———. "Summary of NIH-Specific Provisions in Interim Final Rule, Prohibited Outside Activities." <http://www.nih.gov/about/ethics/020105COIsummary.pdf>

Schellenberg, R. "Sick Minds or Just Human Nature?" *Anorexia Truth.* <http://www
.anorexiatruth.com/display.php?page=Pro-Anorexia%20Web%20Sites>
Treatment Advocacy Center. "Facts on Schizophrenia." <http://www.psychlaws.org/
GeneralResources/Fact5.htm>
United States Department of Agriculture. "Dietary Guidelines for Americans 2005."
<http://www.health.gov/dietaryguidelines/dga2005/document/pdf/DGA2005.pdf>
United States Equal Employment Opportunity Commission, Department of Justice—
Civil Rights Division. "Americans with Disabilities Act: Questions and Answers."
<http://www.usdoj.gov/crt/ada/q%26aeng02.htm>
University of Pittsburgh, Department of Psychiatry. "A Collaborative Study of the
Genetics of Anorexia Nervosa and Bulimia Nervosa." <http://www.wpic.pitt.edu/
research/pfanbn/genetics.html>
University of Pittsburgh Press Release. "University of Pittsburgh to Lead First-Ever
Government-Funded Genetic Study of Anorexia Nervosa." <http://www.wpic.pitt
.edu/research/angenetics/press_release.html>

NEWSPAPER ARTICLES

Clark, Callie. "Cases of Child Autism Have Increased 850 Percent in Missouri." *The
Southeast Missourian.* April 25, 2004.
Loh, Irving Kent, M.D. "Letter to the Editor: Ethics and Unintended Consequences."
Los Angeles Times. February 5, 2005.
Moore, Angela. "Mattel Launches Barbie Clothes for Women." *Reuters News Service.*
New York, 14 October 2005.
"New Rules at NIH Anger its Employees." *Washington Post.* February 4, 2005.
Payne, J. W. "No, That's Sick: Pro-Anorexia Web Site Authors Claim the Condition
is a 'Lifestyle Choice.'" *Washington Post.* 14 September 2004, HE01.
Willman, David. "NIH Seeks 'Higher Standard.'" *Los Angeles Times.* 2 February
2005.

WEB-SITES (ALL WEB-SITES ACCESSED
AS RECENTLY AS JANUARY, 2006)

Academy for Eating Disorders: <http://www.aedweb.org>
American Cancer Society: <http://www.cancer.org/>
American Heart Association: <http://www.americanheart.org/>
American Psychiatric Association: <http://www.psych.org/>
Americans with Disabilities Act: <http://www.ada.gov/>
Anorexia Nervosa and Related Eating Disorders, Inc. (ANRED): <http://www
.anred.com/>
Anorexia Truth: <http://anorexiatruth.com/>

Autistic Society: <http://autisticsociety.org/>

Biophoenix (biomedical consultancy): <http://www.biophoenix.com/>

Centers for Disease Control and Prevention: <http://www.cdc.gov/>

ClinicalTrials.gov: <http://clinicaltrials.gov/>

Computer Retrieval of Information on Scientific Projects (CRISP): <http://crisp.cit.nih.gov/>

Dietary Guidelines for Americans 2005: <http://www.health.gov/dietaryguidelines/dga2005/document/>

Eating Disorders Coalition (EDC): <http://www.eatingdisorderscoalition.org/>

Goliath Casket, Inc. <http://oversizecasket.com>

Harvard Eating Disorders Center (HEDC): <http://www.hedc.org/>

International Diabetes Federation: <http://www.idf.org/>

Joint Commission of Accreditation of Healthcare Organizations (JCAHO): <http://www.jcaho.org/>

Medscape: <http://www.medscape.com/>

MyPyramid.gov: <http://mypyramid.gov>

National Association of Anorexia Nervosa and Associated Disorders (ANAD): <http://www.anad.org/>

The National Cancer Institute (NCI): <http://cis.nci.nih.gov/>

National Center for Injury Prevention and Control: <http://www.cdc.gov/ncipc/>

National Eating Disorders Association (NEDA): <http://www.nationaleatingdisorders.org/>

National Heart, Lung, and Blood Institute: <http://www.nhlbi.nih.gov/>

National Institute of Diabetes and Digestive and Kidney Diseases (NIDDK): <http://www.niddk.nih.gov/>

National Institute of Mental Health (NIMH): <http://www.nimh.nih.gov/>

National Institute of Neurological Disorders and Stroke: <http://www.ninds.nih.gov/>

Preteenagers Today: <http://preteenagerstoday.com/>

Remuda Ranch: <http://www.remuda-ranch.com/>

The Renfrew Center Foundation: <http://www.renfrew.org/>

The Royal College of Psychiatrists: <http://www.rcpsych.ac.uk/>

The Somerset & Wessex Eating Disorders Association: <http://swedauk.org/>

Something Fishy Web-site on Eating Disorders: <http://www.something-fishy.org/>

Treatment Advocacy Center: <http://www.psychlaws.org/>

United States Census Bureau: <http://www.census.gov/>

United States Department of Agriculture: <http://www.usda.gov/wps/portal/usdahome>

University of Pittsburgh School of Medicine, Department of Psychiatry: <http://www.wpic.pitt.edu/>

www.ingramcontent.com/pod-product-compliance
Lightning Source LLC
Chambersburg PA
CBHW021820270326
41932CB00007B/271